JOHN NICHOLSON

John is an Artistic Director of the award-winning Peepolykus, with whom he has toured the UK and the world for twenty-five years. Seven of his stage plays have been published by Nick Hern Books and eight radio plays by BBC Radio 4. His most recent stage play *The Time Machine* was nominated for an Olivier Award.

Writing includes: *The Hound of the Baskervilles* (Leeds Playhouse, West End, national tour), *No Wise Men* (Liverpool Everyman & Playhouse), *Treasure Island*, *King Arthur* (Bristol Old Vic, national tour), *The Massive Tragedy of Madame Bovary* (Northampton Royal, Jermyn Street Theatre, national tour), *A Christmas Carol* (Exeter Northcott), *Spyski – The Importance of Being Honest* (Lyric Hammersmith, national tour), *The Ramsbury Players* (National Theatre), *Richard's Rampage* (The Old Vic, international tour), *Dick Tracy*, *The Three Musketeers* (national tour for Le Navet Bete), *Origins* (Pentabus, national tour), *The Arthur Conan Doyle Appreciation Society* (Edinburgh Traverse), *Help! Get Me Out of This Musical* (South Hill Park), *A Trespasser's Guide to the Classics* (series 1 and 2), *Rik Mayall's Bedside Tales* (series 1), *Marley was Dead* (BBC Radio 4), *Off Their Rockers* (ITV), *The Time Machine* (Original Theatre, national tour).

Physical comedy director/consultant credits include: *One Man, Two Guvnors* (Bolton Octagon, national tour), *A Little Hotel on the Side* (Theatre Royal Bath), *The Secret Adversary* (Newbury Watermill), *Watson and Oliver*, *The Wrong Door* (BBC), *Playtime* (Northampton Royal), *Accidental Death of an Anarchist* (Sheffield Theatres, West End, Olivier nomination).

Directing credits include: *Partners in Crime* (Queens Theatre, Hornchurch), *Dracula – the Bloody Truth*, *400* (Plymouth Theatre Royal/National), *Shaun the Sheep Live* (Aardman/International), *Nina Conti – Dolly Mixtures* (Soho Theatre and West End), *Paul Merton – Out of His Head* (West End), *Spymonkey's Spook Show* (Blackpool Winter Gardens), *Coulrophobia* (London International Mime Festival), *Aladdin*, *Dick Tracy* (Plymouth Athenaeum), *The Three Musketeers* (York Theatre Royal, national tour), *King Arthur* (national tour), *The Light Princess* (Tobacco Factory Theatre, Bristol), *A Christmas Carol* (Exeter Northcott), *Tweedy's Massive Circus* (RSC and national tour), *The Hound of the Baskervilles* (Theatre by the Lake).

LE NAVET BETE

Le Navet Bete is an artist-led theatre company run by company directors Al Dunn, Nick Bunt and Matt Freeman. Since their beginnings in 2008, they have toured the UK and internationally with their unique and chaotic style of physical comedy and have earned the reputation as one of the UK's leading midscale theatre companies, performing at some of the most prestigious venues across the country with an ever-growing and loyal fanbase, an extensive back catalogue of work, and four internationally published scripts. Proudly based in Exeter, Devon, and supported by organisations such as the Exeter Northcott Theatre and the Exeter Phoenix, they have been on a continuous mission to create and tour hilarious, physical and totally accessible comedy theatre using creative and engaging storytelling for absolutely everyone (ages 4 to 104!).

Their first two shows, *Serendipity* and *Zemblanity*, heavily influenced by bouffon and non-narrative structures, were performed at the Edinburgh Festival Fringe in 2008 and 2009 respectively and gained multiple five-star reviews. As the company developed and grew over the following years, their inimitable style of performance became much more storytelling/narrative-driven with hit shows such as *A Christmas Carol*, *The Wonderful Wizard of Oz, Dick Tracy, Dracula: The Bloody Truth, The Three Musketeers: A Comedy Adventure, Treasure Island* and *King Arthur*, placing physical theatre, fooling and slapstick at the heart of it. Since 2020, they have forged a festive partnership with the Exeter Northcott Theatre to write and perform in their annual Christmas show, combining Le Navet Bete's anarchic humour with the classic traditions of pantomime, performing alongside a larger cast.

As well as indoor work, the company diversified into outdoor performance in 2010, quickly becoming one of the UK's most ridiculously outrageous, much-loved outdoor acts, performing to hundreds of thousands from the legendary circus fields at Glastonbury Festival, the beautiful gardens of the Herrenhausen Palace in Hanover, Germany, and a classic yacht festival on the Italian Riviera to the picturesque Plaza de Armas in Morelia, Mexico, an industrial factory in Prague and high up on a cliff on the Rock of Gibraltar.

Le Navet Bete have a widely renowned education programme specialising in clowning, physical comedy, performer–audience relationships and play, that they have taught in schools, colleges and universities across the world from the Royal Central School of Speech and Drama in London to the Universidad Nacional Autonoma de Mexico in Mexico City.

John Nicholson and Le Navet Bete

KING ARTHUR
The Comedy

NICK HERN BOOKS
London
www.nickhernbooks.co.uk

A Nick Hern Book

King Arthur first published in Great Britain in 2024 as a paperback original by Nick Hern Books Limited, The Glasshouse, 49a Goldhawk Road, London W12 8QP, in association with Le Navet Bete

King Arthur copyright © 2024 John Nicholson and Le Navet Bete

John Nicholson and Le Navet Bete have asserted their moral right to be identified as the authors of this work

Cover photography by The Other Richard; artwork by Rebecca Pitt

Designed and typeset by Nick Hern Books, London
Printed in the UK by Mimeo Ltd, Huntingdon, Cambridgeshire PE29 6XX

A CIP catalogue record for this book is available from the British Library

ISBN 978 1 83904 360 4

CAUTION All rights whatsoever in this play are strictly reserved. Requests to reproduce the text in whole or in part should be addressed to the publisher.

Amateur Performing Rights Applications for performance, including readings and excerpts, by amateurs in English should be addressed to the Performing Rights Manager, Nick Hern Books, The Glasshouse, 49a Goldhawk Road, London W12 8QP, *tel* +44 (0)20 8749 4953, *email* rights@nickhernbooks.co.uk, except as follows:

Australia: ORiGiN Theatrical, *email* enquiries@originmusic.com.au, *web* www.origintheatrical.com.au

New Zealand: Play Bureau, 20 Rua Street, Mangapapa, Gisborne, 4010, *tel* +64 21 258 3998, *email* info@playbureau.com

Professional Performing Rights Applications for performance by professionals in any medium and in any language throughout the world should be addressed to Le Navet Bete c/o Exeter Phoenix Arts Centre, Bradninch Place, Gandy Street, Exeter EX4 3LS, tel. +44 (0) 7849 485770, *email* info@lenavetbete.com

Music Backing tracks, scores and sound effects by Jonny Wharton can be obtained and licensed from Nick Hern Books, see details above.

No performance of any kind may be given unless a licence has been obtained. Applications should be made before rehearsals begin. Publication of this play does not necessarily indicate its availability for amateur performance.

www.nickhernbooks.co.uk/environmental-policy

Introduction
John Nicholson

Even if people think they don't know about King Arthur and the legends of Camelot, we all sort of do... somehow. It's like we've absorbed them from a young age without being conscious of it. In fact, the Legends of King Arthur have become a handle for Englishness, despite the fact that they are utterly bonkers. But then again, 'Englishness' and 'bonkers' are pretty synonymous these days, so perhaps the stories are more apposite than ever.

Our starting point for writing this script was to consider how the stories would have originated, and why they have pervaded through the centuries. The first iterations of the legends were written long after King Arthur would have lived. However, in our early writing sessions we gravitated towards the idea that they were spawned in Camelot itself. We then decided it would have taken three pretty desperate and oddball characters to come up with them. And then, in timeless comic tradition, we devised a way to put these characters under pressure. Extreme pressure.

If you are considering staging this production, the actors can, of course, be played by any gender. The actors play Osbert, Edgar and Dave as their main characters, but these names can be changed. Osbert, Edgar and Dave play a number of other characters (including Lancelot, Guinevere and King Arthur), but they also play themselves in disguised versions of Lancelot, Guinevere and King Arthur. We suggest using slightly less good costumes when they are in disguise, but there are plenty of signposts for the audience in the dialogue and so they don't get confused! In the original production there was a great deal of music (which you are welcome to license). The show needs to be played at breakneck speed and requires a great deal of very, very choreographed chaos.

I hope you enjoy the challenge and also the massive liberties we have taken with the source material!

King Arthur was first performed at Queen's Theatre, Barnstaple, on 21 September 2023, before touring the UK. The cast was as follows:

Matt Freeman
Nick Bunt
Al Dunn

Director	John Nicholson
Associate Director	Sophie Cottle
Set & Costume Designer	Fi Russell
Lighting Designer & Technical Manager	Stuart Billinghurst
Composer & Sound Designer	Jonny Wharton
Company Stage Manager	Mel Moran
Assistant Director	Lula Nicholson
Stage Manager	Fi Russell / Jess Crocker
Prop Maker	Lizi Bennett
Costume Supervisor	Jess Riley
Wig Maker	Jess Crocker

Characters

ACTOR 1, *Al*
ACTOR 2, *Nick*
ACTOR 3, *Matt*

EDGAR
OSBERT
DAVE
ARTHUR
JESTER
MR HILL
ACTOR
MERLIN
VIVIANE
LANCELOT
GAWAIN
MORDRED
MORGANA LE FAY
GUINEVERE
PELLINORE
NOBBY
GREEN KNIGHT
BERTILAK
MRS BERTILAK
PERCIVAL
BLACK KNIGHT
GRINGOLET THE HORSE, *voice*
LADY OF SHALOTT
DRAGON
BALYN
BALAN
ITALIAN TAILOR
GUARD

Also STAGE MANAGER

Suggested Doubling

ACTOR 1 – Edgar, Actor, Viviane, Lancelot, Pellinore, Nobby, Mrs Bertilak, Black Knight, Balyn, Italian tailor, Guard.

ACTOR 2 – Osbert, Arthur, Gawain, Mordred, Percival, Lady of Shalott, Balan.

ACTOR 3 – Dave, Jester, Mr Hill, Merlin, Morgana le Fay, Guinevere, Green Knight, Sir Bertilak, Gringolet the Horse, Dragon.

Songs

1. 'I Gotta Get Free'   p. 8
2. 'Mother Son'   p. 38
3. 'The Show Must Continue'   p. 58
4. 'Merlin's Song'   p. 61
5. 'Caravana Morgana'   p. 80
6. 'Let's Rock'   p. 97
7. 'Now I'm a Knight'   p. 102

Backing tracks and vocal scores for the songs by Jonny Wharton can be obtained and licensed from Nick Hern Books.

ACT ONE

Scene One – In the Stocks

Lights up. SFX: a cheering crowd. Three MEN *are in stocks. A fanfare and then a voice comes over the tanoy.*

VOICE. Visitors to Camelot, see ye here before us, three of the utterest buffoonions in the great kingdom of King Arthur. Accused they be of treason. I say 'accused', but let's not beat about the bushel – they're definitely one-hundred-per-cent guilty. So, in the great medieval tradition, I call upon those of you armed with vegetables... yes, that's right, that's you in the front row... take that rotting produce and, on my command, throw it at their stupid faces! Ready... take aim... and fire! Throw it! Now!!

Pre-show, the front row of the audience has been instructed by ushers or STAGE MANAGER (SM) *to throw fake fruit and veg at the* MEN. *Lively music begins with crowd SFX that transitions into a song.*

EDGAR *lifts up his stocks (to free himself to move and sing) on his first line. He is in a pink bodice. He also has a hoover, which he retrieves from the wing during his opening verse, returning it to the* SM *before the next verse.*

EDGAR (*singing*).
  I gotta get free, I gotta get free,
  I gotta get free from this mess
  That I have to confess was all their fault
  I should not be in stocks
  God knows, believe me they're a couple of co–

OSBERT *lifts up his stocks on his first line (to free himself to move and sing and place* EDGAR *back in the stocks). He is in a miniskirt, a white shirt tied at the waist. He twirls a shocking-pink cobweb duster.*

OSBERT (*singing*).
   Cos it wasn't my fault
   It seems that this infernal muddle
   And all of the trouble
   Is patently all down to you two
   That's…
   Unfortunate to be saddled
   With this right pair of tw–

   DAVE *lifts up his stocks on the first line* (*to free himself to move and sing*). *He's naked (flesh-coloured body suit) with a pink crocheted willy.*

DAVE (*singing*).
   'Twas strange but it's true (hey)
   It makes me happy you both love me like you do
   But I think you all know
   And the verdict will show
   I'm all innocent, baby
   I give my stiff guarantee
   So now I gotta get free

   He lands a punch on OSBERT, *which provokes a fight.* EDGAR *rips off* DAVE*'s willy and chucks it into the audience.* DAVE *has to retrieve it. Eventually they all convene to harmonise over…*

ALL (*singing*).
   But life won't go on
   Because we really screwed up
   Really screwed up, really screwed up
   With our show to celebrate Camelot
   God knows
   Perhaps we should've killed Lancelot
   So people, can't you see?
   We gotta break free!

   EDGAR, OSBERT *and* DAVE *position themselves back in the stocks and exit carrying stocks. Instrumental music continues playing.* SM *enters with a sign. It reads 'One week earlier…'*

   SM *then exits.*

Scene Two – Hangover

A farmyard. SFX: pigs and chickens. OSBERT *is in a pig trough.* EDGAR *is passed out then comes to, very hungover.*

EDGAR. Osbert? Dave? Guys, where are you?

No response. EDGAR *fires an arrow at a hanging bucket, which drops and lands on* OSBERT*'s head.* OSBERT *jumps up.*

OSBERT. What the…?! Argh, what happened?

EDGAR. We got drunk and ended up in the pig pen again. Where's Dave?

OSBERT. How should I know? Ow, my head!

EDGAR. That was some night.

OSBERT. Was it? I don't remember a thing.

EDGAR. Me neither.

Pause.

OSBERT. That's not good, is it?

EDGAR. Nope. I don't like the sound of any of this.

OSBERT. Right, let's retrace our steps. The last thing I remember was…

Pause.

BOTH. Dave offering our home-brew beer to the king!

OSBERT. No, no, no!

EDGAR. Oh holy…

DAVE *enters brightly.*

DAVE. Morning, losers! So. Who wants to become a knight?

BOTH. What?

DAVE. A knight.

EDGAR. As in… Knights of the Round Table?

DAVE. Yep. As of last night, 'someone', aka The Davester, secured us three simple squires guaranteed knighthoods in return for just a simple assignment that we can't get out of.

EDGAR. Oh God, what's he agreed to now?

DAVE. Errr... only to turn your sad little lives around.

OSBERT. Dave, how bad is this 'assignment'?

DAVE. It's not bad at all.

EDGAR. How bad?!

DAVE. You'll be thanking me for the rest of your lives.

EDGAR. How bad!?!

Pause.

DAVE. It's pretty bad, but not as bad as your face! He's probably forgotten anyway.

EDGAR. Who has?!

DAVE. The king.

EDGAR/OSBERT. The king?!

DAVE. Although the leaflets have already been printed.

Produces a leaflet.

EDGAR. Give me that!

EDGAR *snatches the leaflet, looks at it and gasps.*

OSBERT. What does it say?

EDGAR. No idea, I can't read.

OSBERT. Give it to me... (*Gasps.*)

EDGAR. What does it say?

OSBERT. I can't read either, actually.

EDGAR *grabs the leaflet back and holds it up to an audience member.*

EDGAR. You. What does it say? Loud and clear.

AUDIENCE. Fifteen per cent off takeaways at The Golden Dragon!

DAVE. Well that's clearly the wrong leaflet – it's this one.

EDGAR. Tell us exactly what happened last night or I swear to God, I'll…

DAVE. Okay! So. You know when Arthur was crowned, he vowed that after a year and a day, he'd hold a grand celebration to broadcast the legacy and stories of Camelot to the world?

EDGAR. ArthurFest. Yes. Terrible idea.

OSBERT. An idea which he was immediately obliged to cancel because there ARE no stories of Camelot.

DAVE. Well after a pint or two… or maybe ten, Arthur confided in me about how depressed he was about the whole situation, so to sort of… buoy him up – and bearing in mind the old brain had clocked off for the night and left 'The Big D' in charge – I promised that we'd help out.

EDGAR. 'We'?!

DAVE. Yeah, it seemed a shame to leave you two out. Hashtag-FOMO.

OSBERT. Of what exactly?!

DAVE. Okay fine. We need to stage a theatre show that will give birth to the legends of King Arthur, ignite fascination in the stories for centuries to come and oddly… become the main reference point for what it means to be English. ArthurFest is back on!

The others are in shock.

I was drunk!! People say stuff when they're drunk!

OSBERT. Yeah, they say stuff like 'I bet I could tip that cow over!' or 'I really fancy your mum!' They don't tell the king they can flip him from zero to hero!

DAVE. You fancy my mum?

EDGAR. No one fancies your mum.

DAVE. My dad did.

OSBERT. Whoever *he* was.

EDGAR. Let's just focus on the king.

DAVE. It definitely wasn't him.

EDGAR. Oh my God! Listen! When you made this ridiculous promise to the king –

DAVE. He said he'd make us knights… if the show works.

OSBERT. And if it didn't?

DAVE. Bog-washing duty for a year.

OSBERT. You have to be KIDDING?! We have to put a stop to this. One: There ARE no stories of Camelot. Two: We can't act –

EDGAR. You can say that again.

OSBERT. And Three: When is this show supposed to happen? Give me that. (*Shows leaflet to audience member.*) You, what does this say? Loud and clear.

AUDIENCE. Have you found Jesus yet?

DAVE. Whoops! That's *definitely* the wrong one.

EDGAR. Why have you got so many leaflets?

DAVE. Got a job as a leaflet-delivery guy. It's this one –

OSBERT (*to audience member*). What does it say?

AUDIENCE. Leaflet-delivery guy needed.

DAVE (*snatches leaflet back*). That's *my* job!

EDGAR. Dave, when is the performance?!

DAVE. Four weeks' time.

EDGAR. Four weeks?!

OSBERT. Unbelievable! I'm going to be sick. (*Quickly exits.*)

EDGAR. I have to put a stop to this. I'm going to go and speak to the king!

DAVE. Well good luck with that. He's very persuasive for a teenager!

EDGAR. Uh. I think I can handle it! Right, off to see the king. How hard can it be? I'm sure he's a reasonable man. Just like I'm a reasonable man. Maybe if I stop walking on the spot I'll actually make it to the castle. Okay, deep breath.

He exits. Instrumental music as the scene changes to Camelot court.

Scene Three – Arthur's Court

ARTHUR *is sat on a wooden throne. A* JESTER *dances on a higher platform.*

ARTHUR. Faster! Bigger! Sillier! Stop! You're embarrassing yourself now. How old are you?

JESTER. Forty.

ARTHUR. Ha! So old. Tell me a joke.

JESTER. That's not really my strong suit.

ARTHUR. Well what is?!

JESTER. Tiling.

ARTHUR. Tiling?!

JESTER. Oh, actually, I do have a joke.

ARTHUR. Good. Make it about me.

JESTER. Right.

ARTHUR. And my sword.

JESTER. Uh, okay.

ARTHUR. And my favourite food.

JESTER. What's your favourite food?

ARTHUR. Omelettes. Go.

JESTER. Okay, hang on… got it. What does King Arthur use to cut his omelettes?

ARTHUR. A knife?

JESTER. No. Eggscalibur!

ARTHUR. Why would I use my sword?! I'd use a knife.

JESTER. No, *Eggs*-calibur.

ARTHUR. Yes, that's my sword.

JESTER. But it's *Eggs*-calibur.

ARTHUR. I know what it's called!

JESTER. It's a joke.

ARTHUR. Are you saying my sword's a joke?

JESTER. No, you're saying it wrong.

ARTHUR. And now you're telling me I can't pronounce the name of my most precious item? Where is Eggscalibur?

JESTER. That's it! Eggscalibur.

ARTHUR. Yes. As in eggs. That you make omelettes with – Eggscalibur. EGGS-calibur… Oh hang on… that's brilliant! (*Laughs a lot, then stops.*) I'm bored now. Next!

EDGAR *appears.*

JESTER. Good luck, mate.

ARTHUR. Right, what can *you* do?

EDGAR. Your Majesty, I am Squire Edgar.

ARTHUR. I couldn't care less.

EDGAR. I believe you met my fellow squire Dave last night…

ARTHUR. Dave! Yes! The Big D! What a funny guy. Oh come on down.

EDGAR *climbs down the ladder and then is forced off the stage.*

Down. Down. Down. Lower. Lower. There we are. The three saviours of Camelot. I shall forever be indebted to you!

EDGAR. Yes, well about that. Despite your generous offer of knighthoods, I'm afraid that we're obliged to cancel our 'show' and withdraw from our 'agreement'. So we wish you the very best of luck for ArthurFest.

ARTHUR. No.

EDGAR. I'm afraid so.

ARTHUR. No!

EDGAR. Please?

ARTHUR. The invitations have gone out and the world shall hear the legendary stories of Camelot.

EDGAR. Which identifies the problem: *what* legendary stories?

ARTHUR. That's what you're going to solve!

EDGAR. Sire, I must insist, there's been a big misunderstanding here.

ARTHUR. No. You can't do this to me. (*Starts to get upset.*) I mean, ArthurFest?! Whose idea was that anyway?!

EDGAR. Yours?

ARTHUR. It was just bants! And now it's real life. What am I going to do? I'm ruined.

He collapses to his knees in a mess. EDGAR *attempts to raise his spirits.*

EDGAR. Sire… I'm sure it will be fine.

ARTHUR *jumps up, fully restored.*

ARTHUR. Great. And you know there are big rewards for the three of you.

EDGAR. No, hang on. I didn't mean that –

ARTHUR. But if you embarrass me, you will be sentenced to death and your silly little heads placed on spikes. Sad face.

EDGAR. I thought it was just 'toilet duty for a year'?!

ARTHUR. It was. But your visit has just raised the stakes. I have every faith in you, Egghead.

EDGAR. Edgar.

ARTHUR *gives him a huge bear-hug.*

ARTHUR. One of my closest friends. Best friends forever. Pinkie promise.

ARTHUR *holds out his little finger until* EDGAR *does the same.* ARTHUR *then sucks* EDGAR*'s little finger.*

That's more like it. I know you won't let me down.

ARTHUR *exits.*

EDGAR. Oh crap!

He's suddenly back in the farmyard. Instrumental music. DAVE *enters.*

Scene Four – The Farmyard: 'You've Killed Us Now'

DAVE. Did you see him? Did you tell him I'm an idiot?

EDGAR. Yep.

DAVE. And there's no way we can deliver?

EDGAR. Yep.

DAVE. And what did he say?

EDGAR. He started crying.

DAVE. Crying? Did he suck your finger?

EDGAR. Yeah.

DAVE. I taught him that.

OSBERT *enters.*

EDGAR. He said he'd put our heads on spikes if we embarrassed him.

OSBERT. And what did you say?

EDGAR. I hugged him.

OSBERT. Oh my God!

DAVE. It was only bog-washing duty last night!

OSBERT. So basically you've killed us now!

EDGAR. Hey, it was Dave that got us into this!

OSBERT. Unbelievable! Like… unfathomably unbelievable! Look, I'll go and speak to him.

EDGAR. Don't. It won't work.

DAVE. You'll only make it worse.

OSBERT. How could I *possibly* make this any worse?!

OSBERT *exits.*

Scene Five – The Farmyard (Continued)

Lightning-quick instrumental music and lighting transition.
OSBERT *enters.*

OSBERT. I made it worse.

EDGAR. You see!

DAVE. What happened?

OSBERT. He just kept asking me what he should use to cut up his omelettes.

DAVE. And what did you say?

OSBERT. A knife.

DAVE. And what did he say?

OSBERT. His sword.

DAVE. Random? Then what?

OSBERT. He just kept saying Eggscalibur.

DAVE. You mean *Ex*-calibur?

OSBERT. That's what I said.

DAVE. No, you said *Eggs*-calibur.

OSBERT. I know.

DAVE. But it's *Ex*-calibur.

OSBERT. I know.

DAVE. So why are you saying *Eggs*-calibur.

OSBERT. Because that's the name of his sword.

DAVE. Listen!! You're saying *Eggs*-calibur. As in eggs. Eggs that you make omelettes out of. Oh hang on that is absolutely brilliant.

OSBERT. Jesus, this is the same bloody loop I got into with the king.

EDGAR. And how did it end?

OSBERT. He punched me in the face.

EDGAR. Like this?

ACT ONE, SCENE FIVE

EDGAR *punches* OSBERT *in the face.*

OSBERT. No, more like this.

OSBERT *goes to punch him but* EDGAR *has moved* DAVE *into position, so* OSBERT *punches* DAVE.

EDGAR. What happened next?

OSBERT. He kicked me up the arse.

DAVE. Like this?

DAVE *kicks* OSBERT *up the arse.*

OSBERT. No, more like this

OSBERT *kicks* DAVE *up the arse.*

EDGAR. And then what?

OSBERT. I kicked *him* up the arse.

DAVE. Like this?

DAVE *kicks* OSBERT *up the arse.*

EDGAR. Then what?

OSBERT. He kicked *himself* up the arse.

DAVE. Like this?

DAVE *attempts to kick himself up the arse and falls over.*

DAVE. It's not possible.

EDGAR. How did you make it worse?!

OSBERT. Just a slight amendment to the performance date.

EDGAR. As in…

OSBERT. It's been put forward by three weeks.

EDGAR. Three weeks?! That only leaves us with a week until the show!

OSBERT. I know! There's only one thing for it.

EDGAR. No! No more ideas!

OSBERT. We run away.

EDGAR. Apart from that one. That's good.

DAVE. Absolutely not, we do *not* run away from our problems. That's *not* how my mother raised me. You know what she said to me on my sixteenth birthday?

OSBERT. That she would've been better off giving birth to a can opener?

DAVE. After that.

EDGAR. Listen! If we don't do the show, we die. If we do it, which is impossible, we also die. Our only option is to –

DAVE. Eat each other.

The others stare blankly at DAVE.

What were you going to say?

EDGAR. Run to the hills.

DAVE. Let's go with that.

EDGAR. Right. So, we run to the hills and hide up. We wait until this whole thing has blown over, then we change our identities and start new lives.

DAVE. Already on it. Basically, I move to a Balearic island, get a mother lode of glow sticks, buy some decks and say hello to 'Sir Dave the Rave'! Eat, sleep, rave, repeat… (*Improvise DJ routine.*)

EDGAR *smacks him over the head with a frying pan.*

EDGAR. Ready?

OSBERT. Let's go.

BOTH. To the hills!

Scene Six – Run to the Hills

Iron Maiden's 'Run to the Hills' kicks in. Choreographed running routine. During this, DAVE *exits.* EDGAR *and* OSBERT *end up standing in front of a door.*

OSBERT. Right, here we are. Mr and Mrs Hill's house.

OSBERT *knocks. Top of stable door opens.*

EDGAR. Hello, Mr Hill.

MR HILL. Oh no, not you idiots again.

OSBERT. We were wondering if we could come and live with you for a little bit.

MR HILL. With me? And Mrs Hill? And all the little Hillocks? Are you 'avin' a giraffe?! No. Sling your 'ook!

Slams door.

OSBERT. Well that was a bad idea. Where do we try next?

EDGAR. The Woods'?

OSBERT. No, they've only got a bungalow.

EDGAR. The Marshes'?

OSBERT. They've moved.

EDGAR. Where to?

OSBERT. The Cliffs'.

EDGAR. So where have the Cliffs gone?

OSBERT. The Fields'.

EDGAR. And the Fields?

OSBERT. Sad story.

EDGAR. Died?

OSBERT. Got built on.

EDGAR. How about the Churches?

OSBERT. Bit draughty.

EDGAR. Maidenhead?

OSBERT. Birkenhead!

EDGAR. Knobhead!

OSBERT. Wait, I'm confused, what the hell are we talking about?!

EDGAR. No idea.

OSBERT. And where's Dave?

DAVE (*entering*). Who?

He's made EDGAR *jump.*

EDGAR. Oh for Pete's sake.

DAVE/OSBERT. Who's Pete?

EDGAR. Right, we either stay here in this stupid topographical surname routine, OR... (*Big epic dramatic moment.*) We return to Camelot. We put on the greatest show the world has ever seen, be ordained Knights of the Round Table and change the course of history forever. Gentlemen, the choice is now yours.

DAVE. The first one. The surname routine

EDGAR. No, we have to do the show. Choose again.

DAVE. Stay here. One hundred per cent.

EDGAR (*as in: 'Do the honours'*). Osbert?

OSBERT punches DAVE in the face.

Back to the farmyard?

OSBERT. Back to the farmyard!

Slightly off version of 'Old Macdonald' kicks in. EDGAR *and* OSBERT *transition across the stage in tiny, rapid footsteps.* DAVE *walks normally.*

Scene Seven – Embarking on the Play

They arrive back at the farmyard.

OSBERT. Okay, here we are. Six days till ArthurFest. Putting on the play: *the world of acting*. What do we know about that?

EDGAR. About as much as Dave knows about personal hygiene.

DAVE. Personal what?

EDGAR. I rest my case.

Pause.

OSBERT. Right. That's that out of the way.

DAVE. Brilliant. We're racing through this.

EDGAR. No. We need to learn how to act.

OSBERT. How?

DAVE. Ask an actor?

OSBERT. Makes sense.

DAVE. Sweet. Let's take a pew.

EDGAR. What – we just wait for one to stroll on by?!

DAVE. Unless you've got a better idea?!

DAVE *sits.* OSBERT *joins him.* EDGAR *looks incredulous.*

EDGAR. Right, you pair of flip-flops can stay here. I'm gonna go and do a mobile search.

EDGAR *exits.*

Scene Eight – An Actor Arrives

OSBERT. I think we've got more chance of an actor strolling by with him gone.

DAVE. Yeah. (*Pause.*) How'd you work that one out?

OSBERT shares his exasperation with the audience and begins to explain using his fingers. DAVE falls asleep. From off we hear a recorder playing – approaching.

OSBERT. Dave! Wake up!

DAVE. Badgers! What's going on?

OSBERT. Actor, two o'clock. Quick.

An ACTOR enters. They hide.

He must have broken away from his ensemble.

DAVE (*heading towards him, knife in hand*). Follow me.

OSBERT. Hang on, why have you got a knife?!

DAVE. In case I want an omelette.

They approach.

ACTOR. Ah, finally. My audience. Please take your seats, the show is about to begin. I am Bill Spollock; travelling bard. Good sirs, what will you have me perform – a soliloquy, a sonnet, a ballad perhaps?

OSBERT. No Bill Spollock. You must help us. We have to learn how to act.

ACTOR. Ha! You wish to tread the boards, join the noblest profession in the land? You must sign up to my twelve-week workshop.

OSBERT. We haven't got time for all that, Spollocks. We need a crash course.

ACTOR. There are no short cuts. (*He holds up a book.*) It took me ten years of studying *The Acting Bible* to become this affected.

OSBERT. Okay, we'll buy it off you.

ACTOR. Oh, I don't think so. This is my only copy. My lifeblood. I shall never part with it.

DAVE. Hand it over!

He holds the knife up.

The ACTOR *suddenly breaks into a death performance, as if he's been stabbed. Dramatic music, red ribbons for blood, etc., until falling to the ground.*

ACTOR. Yea, noise? Then I'll be brief. O happy dagger! This is thy sheath; there rust, and let me die.

He dies.

OSBERT. What have you done?! You killed him.

DAVE. I wasn't anywhere near him!

OSBERT. So how do you explain *this*?! The ground is soaked with his blood!

DAVE. It looks a little bit like red ribbons.

OSBERT. Who has red ribbon coming out of their body?! Just grab the book!

DAVE *grabs the book and they quickly exit. The* ACTOR *stands and reveals the real book.*

ACTOR. Oh dear. It would appear that my acting skills have yet again won the day! Thank you all for your rapturous applause!

He bows excessively to the audience.

Thank you, thank you! You're too kind. I have been Bill Spollock and I will be appearing in rep on a wooden stage near you.

He exits.

Scene Nine – The Book of Acting

The location changes and OSBERT *and* DAVE *appear somewhere else on set.*

DAVE *has the book.*

OSBERT. Right, what does it say?

DAVE. It seems to be some kind of Spanish cookbook!

OSBERT. How did you work that one out?

DAVE. It's full of pictures of tapas.

OSBERT. Those are taps, you idiot!

DAVE. Okay, so it's a plumbing manual! Either way it's the wrong bloody book. Where are you going?

OSBERT. We have to get the real book! We'll have to go back to the murder scene now!

They exit. EDGAR *enters with a book.* OSBERT *and* DAVE *enter and start manically looking around.*

Oh God, he's gone.

EDGAR. Who's gone?

OSBERT. Dave killed an actor.

DAVE. I wasn't anywhere near him!

OSBERT. Hang on, what's that?

EDGAR. This, you pair of plums, is *The Acting Bible*. I got it off an actor.

DAVE. Hang on... describe this actor.

EDGAR. Blue cape, red beret, playing a recorder.

DAVE. That's Bill Spollock! I didn't kill him!

OSBERT. Then how do you explain his blood on the floor!

Picks up a big piece of red material.

EDGAR. That's not blood, you idiot. It's a Fuzzy-Felt cut-out. Look. Page twenty-two. Stage-blood hacks!

ACT ONE, SCENE NINE

DAVE. Hang on, he just gave you the book?

EDGAR. Yeah. After I lopped his head off.

He does the movement.

DAVE. And it just came off?

EDGAR. It surprised me too if I'm honest.

OSBERT. Wait! Look at this. Page forty-one. Fake heads!

ALL. 'Kinell!

EDGAR. He must have scarpered after I left him for dead. With his little boy.

OSBERT. What little boy?

EDGAR. So high, flappy arms and legs, had to be dragged.

DAVE *is looking at the book.*

DAVE. Expressionless hessian face?

EDGAR. Yes.

DAVE. Marbles for eyes?

EDGAR. Now that you mention it!!

DAVE. Extendable wooden nose?

EDGAR. I'm not lying, Dave!

DAVE. Puppets!! Look. There's a whole chapter on the bloody things! We've been had!!

OSBERT. Who cares? (*Takes book.*) We are now in possession of the only thing that might save our lives. Boys, this book must be devoured. We inhale every page, every lesson, every illustration, every word.

EDGAR. How? There's not enough time.

OSBERT. With a montage.

Montage music starts. DAVE *and* OSBERT *begin to strike various montage poses.*

EDGAR. Whoa whoa whoa! Stop.

Montage music abruptly stops.

There's just one other thing.

OSBERT. What?

EDGAR. We can't read.

OSBERT. Damn! Okay, we need a book on how to read.

DAVE. As luck would have it, I've got one right here.

EDGAR. Great, what does it say?

DAVE. No idea, it's just pictures of taps.

OSBERT. That's tapas!

EDGAR. Why have you got a Spanish cookbook?

DAVE. No entiendo.

OSBERT. Shut up! It doesn't matter. This is getting ridiculous. From now on, we can read… end of. Go, montage!

We hear the ACTOR*'s voice listing the following chapter headings. After each chapter heading,* EDGAR, OSBERT *and* DAVE *mime a brief routine in explanation of each one* (*like, a ten-second snap shot of each*).

ACTOR (*voice-over*). Chapter One: Facing the Right Way.

Chapter Two: Singing.

Chapter Three: Stage Combat.

Chapter Four: Puppets.

Emotions: Happy, Sad, Angry, Constipation.

Mime.

Acrobatics!

They celebrate the completion of their training.

Scene Ten – How Are We Going to Do It?

Back at the farmyard.

EDGAR. We've done it.

OSBERT. Lads, we're now level-one actors!

EDGAR. Right, only five days till ArthurFest. What's next?

OSBERT. Act out the stories of Camelot.

DAVE. Of which there are none.

OSBERT. Yet. Who are the significant personalities?

EDGAR. Let's make a list; Merlin, his girlfriend Viviane, Guinevere, Arthur's mates the knights – Gawain, Lancelot, Balyn and Balan. His half-sister Morgana, her son Mordred and a couple of others that most people haven't heard of.

OSBERT. Hang on, we might be able to act but we're just a cast of three! How are we going to portray all those people?

DAVE (*holding up* The Acting Bible). Guys, we missed a chapter. Look. Page ninety-seven. (*Reads.*) 'Multi-roling – a style of theatre where an actor plays multiple characters by adjusting costume, voice and physical appearance.'

OSBERT. No way. That's next-level stuff.

DAVE. Have faith. We can do it.

EDGAR. Are you seriously trying to suggest there are people out there who would pay good money to watch the three of us attempting to play a dozen or so characters? Each?

DAVE. Listen! If we can pull this off, think how much respect we'd earn. Think of the beers they'd buy us in the bar afterwards.

They all look at the audience.

EDGAR. I'm in!

OSBERT. Me too. Right, we have to tap up all the people on that list for their stories. Surely *something* exciting has happened in the last twelve months! Who's going to visit the knights?

EDGAR. Oof, the knights have swords. They could literally kill us.

OSBERT. I'm not going, no way.

EDGAR. Me neither! Here, watch this. Dave?

DAVE. Yeah?

EDGAR. You go and see Lancelot and all the other knights.

DAVE. Yeah.

DAVE exits.

EDGAR. Merlin's another obvious place to start – what with him being keeper of the records of Camelot.

OSBERT. I'll take him and these three, you take the next three.

EDGAR. Godspeed, Osbert.

EDGAR exits.

OSBERT. Godspeed. Right. Off to see the legendary Merlin.

OSBERT makes a journey and arrives at MERLIN*'s door. He knocks.*

Scene Eleven – Merlin's Gaff

Lots of smoke. MERLIN *is backlit – we see what seems to be a mystical figure concocting a spell over a cauldron. The music swells epically until the lights come up and he's revealed boiling his pants, wearing a dressing gown and slippers.*

OSBERT. Excuse me? Merlin?

MERLIN (*spinning around*). Viviane?! Someone's trying to steal our laundry!

OSBERT. No, no. You misunderstand. My name is Osbert.

MERLIN. I didn't do it!

OSBERT. Do what?

MERLIN. Doesn't matter.

OSBERT. I was wondering whether you could share any exciting stories of Camelot?

MERLIN (*picking up a pack of cards*). Pick a card. Any card.

OSBERT. I haven't actually got masses of time so...

MERLIN (*shouting*). Pick a card, man! No, not that one. The one I'm forcing you to pick. Now place it back in the pack, Now, I'll give them a quick shuffle

He drops the entire pack into the laundry pot. He rolls up one of his sleeves and shoves in a hand. There is a scalding hiss. MERLIN *holds up a pair of pants.*

Is this it? Ah no, those are my pants. Viviane!

VIVIANE *appears on the platform above. She's holding a large sack.*

VIVIANE. I didn't do it!

MERLIN. We have a guest.

VIVIANE. A guess? Very well. Seven of spades.

MERLIN. No. A guest.

VIVIANE. I've had a test.

MERLIN. A guest! He wants stories.

VIVIANE. I'm coming down.

MERLIN. Oh boy, here we go. She can't use stairs. She's like a cow. No problem getting up them but completely useless getting down.

VIVIANE *attempts to get down off the platform but ends up facing the wrong way on* MERLIN*'s shoulders.*

VIVIANE. I'm flying!

MERLIN *places* VIVIANE *on her back on the lower platform and then pushes her to her feet. She runs off (and back up the stairs).*

MERLIN. You watch. She'll be straight back up those stairs like a rat up a drainpipe. This routine goes on all day long, you know. And you can imagine the fallout from the exertion – we both cack ourselves. That accounts for all the boiling pants you see. This is my life. That and a little bit of tabletop magic.

He pulls flowers from his sleeve.

OSBERT. Maybe I'll just come back another time. Watch out!

VIVIANE *is back on the platform and about to fall.*

MERLIN. I've got you!

MERLIN *helps her down again.*

We love living in the lake. *On* the lake. *By* the lake!

OSBERT. By the lake, right.

VIVIANE. I'm flying to the moon!

MERLIN *places* VIVIANE *back on the floor. She runs off back up the stairs.*

MERLIN. If you want stories, she's the one with the stories.

OSBERT. Stories? Really?

MERLIN. Oh yes. She's been all over Wales you know. Nice people, the Welsh. They gave her an elephant.

OSBERT. And where does she keep that?

MERLIN. In her sack. She's been to France too. They gave her a giraffe.

OSBERT. In the sack?

MERLIN. In the sack. Chinese gave her a tiger.

OSBERT. Sack?

MERLIN. Are you mad?! It's in a cage.

OSBERT. And where's the cage?

MERLIN. In the sack!

MERLIN *instinctively turns to grab* VIVIANE, *who is about to fall off again.*

Right, I think it's time for us to go on in. Help me close the door there, young chap. Time for tea and cakes.

OSBERT *pushes the door and* VIVIANE *is trapped in the room with* MERLIN. *He pokes his head through the slider in the door.*

I hope you got everything you needed.

OSBERT. No, not really.

MERLIN. She's not all bad you know. She's incredibly good at… not now, Viviane…

His face contorts with weird pleasure.

Scrabble!

The slider quickly slams shut.

OSBERT. Well, that was a complete waste of time. I hope Dave's having more luck with Lancelot.

He exits. Scene transition music – French-café style.

Scene Twelve – Lancelot and Gawain

Lights up in a new location. A kitchen countertop has been set up. From offstage we hear lots of commotion and shouting, pots and pans clattering.

LANCELOT (*off*). You do not know who you are dealing with! I am the fearless Lancelot; Knight of the Round Table.

LANCELOT *enters his kitchen wearing parts of a knight outfit with an apron over the top. He's very French.*

Call yourself a catering service?! Mon dieu. Now I will have to change the entire menu for ArthurFest. Gawain?!

GAWAIN *pops up from behind the counter. He's like a reformed East End gangster.*

GAWAIN. Who needs sorting out?

LANCELOT. How am I supposed to cook without the proper ingredients? I am like a fisherman without a rurrrd, a gardener without a fooook.

GAWAIN. Lance, mate, calm down. Remember what you've taught me.

DAVE *enters.*

DAVE. Sir Lancelot? Sir Gawain? Big up, massive respect. It's the Davester in the house. Your house.

LANCELOT. You! Shut up. Try this – (*Shoves a spoon in his mouth.*) More salt?

GAWAIN (*threatening with a meat cleaver*). What's your business?

DAVE. The king's commissioned a performance for ArthurFest – *The Legends of King Arthur.*

LANCELOT. What legends?

DAVE. Yeah, that's the old problemo.

LANCELOT. Oh, you think you 'ave 'problemos'?! We're supposed to be presenting a live cook-along show for ArthurFest and we only have days to perfect the menu! Gawain, put him to work.

GAWAIN *hands* DAVE *a whisk in a bowl and a crate to sit on.*

GAWAIN. Sit. Now you take care of that. (*Emotional.*) That's a very special whisk. I love that whisk! Sorry, carry on, Lance, mate.

LANCELOT. Bonjour, everyone. Today we are making coq au vin. (*To* DAVE.) Stir, David! Stiffy peaks!

DAVE. But could I just ask you about some stories –

GAWAIN (*threateningly points a piping bag at* DAVE). Do not interrupt Chef Lancelot.

LANCELOT. It's fine, Gawain. I can mooltitask.

GAWAIN. Okay, go ahead.

DAVE. So, I get the vibes that you guys are well into like… food and stuff?

LANCELOT. It's all I live for.

GAWAIN. It's all he lives for! Works all the hours God sends. You know what time he gets up? Tell him.

ACT ONE, SCENE TWELVE   35

LANCELOT. Eleven o'clock.

GAWAIN. Six a.m.! Even on a Sunday.

DAVE. Right. But in France, you must have built a reputation for saving fair maidens?

LANCELOT. There's only one thing I'm interested in saving.

GAWAIN. One thing!

LANCELOT. People's tastebuds.

GAWAIN. Their 'kin tastebuds!

DAVE. Right. So what's your deal, Gawain?

GAWAIN. No. I won't talk of the past.

LANCELOT. You must, Gawain! Step Twelve. Forgive and Forget!

GAWAIN. Very well. I was consumed with battle lust. When Lancelot found me I was…

He's emotional.

LANCELOT. Let it oot, Gawain.

GAWAIN. …fighting a massive bag of cement.

LANCELOT. He was mortified. But I turned all that around.

GAWAIN. Duck ravioli with truffle foam! Never tasted anything like it.

LANCELOT. Stick oot your toooooong.

LANCELOT *dumps a teaspoon into* DAVE's *mouth.*

DAVE. Wow, that really is…

LANCELOT. I know. So less of the yakety-yakety-yak and more of the mmmmm. Now swallow.

DAVE. Wow! Hang on though! I mean, you're still knights! What if someone ran at you with a sword?

LANCELOT. Beluga caviar in a dook-egg yook! Stops anyone in their tracks.

DAVE. But there must be something heroic that's happened?! A bear? A giant?!

GAWAIN. There *was* a giant bear.

LANCELOT. Ah, oui! The damsel of Shalott trapped by a giant bear, in fact.

DAVE. That's more like it. What happened?

LANCELOT. The bear came running towards me.

GAWAIN. Running towards him!

DAVE. Here we go.

LANCELOT. I drew my sword…

GAWAIN. He drew his sword, he did!

DAVE. And then what?!

LANCELOT. I turned that bear into a beautiful casserool!

GAWAIN. 'Kin beautiful. There's your story.

DAVE. Yeah. (*Beat.*) It's not exactly a classic, is it?

GAWAIN. Yes it is – (*Getting emotional.*) it's epic, the stuff of legends.

LANCELOT. Did you get everything you wanted for your show?

DAVE. No.

LANCELOT. Gawain, I think there's some casserool left out the back. Get David a little doogy bag.

GAWAIN. Yes, Chef. Follow me.

They exit.

LANCELOT. Ah finally, it's just you and me, coq. Okay, Lance-a-coq, I mean -lot, time to show them what you're made of. But first, who would like a French Fancy?

Heads into the audience and starts handing out cakes.

Yes I am coming down. Here we go, madame, would you like a French Fancy? Or do you fancy a Frenchie? Haha, I yolk! Now back to my prep, au revoir!

He exits. Instrumental music and transition to…

Scene Thirteen – Morgana and Mordred's Medieval Caravan

MORDRED *is sitting, playing a simple ball-and-cup game in front of the exterior of a beautifully ornate caravan with 'Morgana's' painted on the outside.* MORGANA *enters, singing to herself.*

MORGANA. Mordred! Stop slouching.

MORDRED. Sorry, Mother.

MORGANA. Just because we're forced to live in a caravan rather than a castle doesn't mean we have to let our standards drop. You're destined for big things, my boy.

MORDRED. What big things?

MORGANA. Well for a start, you're next in line for the throne.

MORDRED. Exactly. Next in line. Uncle Arthur would have to die first for anything exciting to happen in my life.

MORGANA. That's not what I meant. And surely you wouldn't wish your own father dead?

MORDRED. Sorry? Father?

MORGANA. I MEAN UNCLE!!

EDGAR *enters.*

EDGAR. Excuse me. Morgana le Fay? My name is Squire Edgar and I'm seeking exciting stories of Camelot.

MORGANA. Well you've come to the right place, Squire Edgar, because this boy right here is destined to rule the world. Hit it!

Intro to song begins.

EDGAR. What's going on?

MORDRED. Mother no, please. This is so embarrassing!

MORGANA. Oh Mordred, stop being such a teenager.

MORDRED. But *I am* a teenager.

MORGANA. Yes, but you're not like other boys your age.

(*Singing.*)
This boy, is truly the love of my life
And
I'm certain that
He will never leave me for a wife

MORDRED (*singing*).
That's true to an extent
And although that's
So well meant
I must be free, to spread my wings
I want to cut these apron strings
Muck about, do teenage things
Like sit in doubt and be depressed
Have sexy thoughts and think of breasts

MORGANA (*singing*).
I hear you, son, but listen to me
You're the next in line and you could be
The greatest king to ever rule the world

I'm your mother

MORDRED (*singing*).
And I'm your son!

MORGANA (*singing*).
I'm your mother

MORDRED (*singing*).
And I'm your son!

BOTH (*singing*).
Mother, son,
Mother, son,
Yeah!

EDGAR. Look, sorry to butt in but…

They force EDGAR *into the choreography.*

MORDRED (*singing*).
Mother, if you want an honest relationship
I'm warning you
You must start by telling me the truth

MORGANA (*singing*).
Okay, I guess it will all come out some time
It's so unclear
I'm not sure if your uncle is
Your father or if you are his
Son or nephew, it's such a tizz
And I am so utterly
Confused by all the history

During the chorus MORDRED, *shocked, asks questions like 'Is Arthur my dad? Or my uncle?'*

Mother, son,
Mother, son,
Mother, son,
Mother, son,
Mother, son,
Mother, son,
Yeah!

MORDRED *exits, crying.*

(*Spoken.*) Did you get everything you wanted?

EDGAR. I certainly got something.

MORGANA. And so did I. Great! See you!

Instrumental music. They both exit.

Scene Fourteen – Have We Got Any Stories?

Back at the farmyard.

OSBERT. Right, what have we got? ANY good stories of Camelot?

EDGAR. Nope. Total disaster. Morgana is… well, 'dysfunctional family' doesn't even come close. You?

OSBERT. Merlin's off-the-scale nuts.

EDGAR. And his girlfriend?

OSBERT. What, Viviane? I literally don't have the words. What about Lancelot? Where's Dave?

A hatch opens in the toilet door.

DAVE. Toilet. Don't ask. Dodgy bear casserole.

Toilet SFX.

OSBERT. That's it. We're at the end of the road, lads. Four days to go and we've got nada. No show. It's gonna be a no-show show.

EDGAR. Unless… we appeal to the only person Arthur might listen to. Guinevere.

They melt.

BOTH. Guinevere.

OSBERT. I'll go.

EDGAR. I'll go.

OSBERT. I'll go.

OSBERT and EDGAR fight.

EDGAR. Fine! We'll both go.

Instrumental music. They go.

Scene Fifteen – Meeting Guinevere

EDGAR *and* OSBERT *arrive.* GUINEVERE *is relaxing on a swing without a care in the world.*

GUINEVERE. Ooh, a couple of squire boys. Hello.

BOTH. Hello, Guinevere.

GUINEVERE. Why so twitchy?

OSBERT. Well, you see the thing is, it's like this –

GUINEVERE. Relax. Take it slowly.

EDGAR. We've got ourselves into a bit of a mess.

GUINEVERE. That sounds unfortunate. Perhaps a nice cool glass of chocolate milkshake with whipped cream dripping with caramel syrup would help?

OSBERT. With a long banana in it?

EDGAR. Osbert, snap out of it! I'm afraid that we don't have time for that, my lady. You see, we've promised the king that we're going to make Camelot exalted.

GUINEVERE. Oh yes, I've heard. He's so excited.

OSBERT. But the thing is –

EDGAR. We can't.

OSBERT. So we wondered whether you, his most trusted confidante, might talk to him and tell him how impossible the challenge actually is. Because otherwise you see, we might…

EDGAR. Die. Definitely die. And someone as fair and kind-hearted as you wouldn't want that, would you?

GUINEVERE. Okay, this is what I think I should do.

She thinks.

OSBERT (*aside*). She's gonna help us.

EDGAR (*aside*). She actually might!

GUINEVERE. I think I should ask the guards to round you up and have you tortured.

EDGAR. No. No! That really won't be necessary because –

GUINEVERE. Because?

OSBERT. We're going to put the play on. And it's going to be amazing.

EDGAR. Incredible.

GUINEVERE. Oh great. I can't wait to see what gems you come up with.

EDGAR. Yes!

OSBERT. Yes. Thank you so much!

They exit. GUINEVERE *signals to begin 'Milkshake' by Kelis. She jumps down from where she is sitting and knocks on the door behind her. A shutter opens and she's handed a milkshake. She takes a long sip and exits.*

Scene Sixteen – Mistaken Identity

EDGAR. Right, well that couldn't have gone any worse!

OSBERT. How does she do it?

EDGAR. Manage to be so fearful and seductive all at the same time?

OSBERT. Exactly. And we've only got three days till ArthurFest!

EDGAR. How did *that* take a day?

OSBERT. I don't know, I don't control the planets, do I?! Where's Dave?

EDGAR. Who?

OSBERT. Dave!!

EDGAR. Oh! Sorry, it's just such a strange name.

DAVE *enters from the 'toilet'.*

DAVE. So, what happened?

EDGAR. There's about as much chance of Guinevere talking the king round as… you impersonating her and talking the king round.

DAVE *has just been handed a golden ticket. Eventually the others notice him.*

OSBERT. Seriously?! You? Passing yourself off as Guinevere?! Don't make me laugh!

DAVE. Watch this space.

He exits. They laugh. Hilarious.

ACT ONE, SCENE SIXTEEN

OSBERT. It's official. He's lost it! That is, without doubt, the most berserk and delusional notion he's ever had.

EDGAR. Can you imagine what would happen if he did present himself to the king, trying to pass himself off as Guinevere?

OSBERT. Hung, drawn and quartered. No question.

EDGAR. No question.

OSBERT. Right. So without any stories, where are we at?

EDGAR. Dead.

DAVE *enters dressed as* GUINEVERE.

DAVE. Hello, squires.

EDGAR *and* OSBERT *get down on one knee, completely fooled.*

OSBERT. My lady?

EDGAR. My lady.

DAVE. I've been thinking. I've changed my mind. I will go and see the king and tell him to cancel your show at ArthurFest. Good day, gentlemen.

DAVE (*as* GUINEVERE) *exits.*

EDGAR. That didn't just happen!

OSBERT. Er… I think it just did!! What made her change her mind?

EDGAR. Who cares. We're off the hook?!

OSBERT. We can't be.

EDGAR. Oh yes we can be! We have to tell Dave.

OSBERT. Oh. My. God!

DAVE *re-enters.*

OSBERT. Dave! You won't believe what just happened?

DAVE. Er… Guinevere's changed her mind?

EDGAR. Yes. How do you know that?

DAVE. Cos it was me dressed as Guinevere, you total dummies!

They both look at DAVE *like he's mad.*

EDGAR. Oh shut up, Dave, you plank. (*Back to* OSBERT.) So, do you reckon she'll head straight to the king?

OSBERT. It didn't sound like she was gonna hang around.

EDGAR. We've just got to hope nothing throws a spanner in the works.

DAVE. Guys, it was me dressed as Guinevere!

EDGAR. Will you give it a rest?

DAVE. Right, fine! You two can do what you want but I'm dressing up as Guinevere and heading off to see the king to get us off the hook.

OSBERT. Don't you even think about it.

OSBERT *hits him with a frying pan.* DAVE *takes the pan and hits him back.* OSBERT *goes down.* EDGAR *takes the pan and hits* DAVE. DAVE *takes the pan and hits* EDGAR. EDGAR *goes down.*

DAVE (*in a faux-Guinevere voice*). 'Right. Off to the castle.'

Instrumental music. DAVE *exits.* OSBERT *and* EDGAR *come to.*

OSBERT. Oh no. How long have we been out?

EDGAR. A day?

OSBERT. What?! That means we've only got two days till ArthurFest!

EDGAR. Wait, where's Dave?

OSBERT. No. He can't be heading to see Arthur. Whenever Dave gets a plan in his head there is no stopping him. What do we do?!

EDGAR. Uh… got it! Got it. Have you ever seen my party trick?

OSBERT. Yes and I was scarred for life.

EDGAR. Not that one, my impression of Lancelot! Listen. 'Who would like a French Fancy?'

ACT ONE, SCENE SEVENTEEN   45

OSBERT. Wow, that's uncanny!

EDGAR. Thanks. So here's the plan: I disguise myself as Lancelot and catch up with Dave.

OSBERT. Okay. And?

EDGAR. Me, passing myself off as Lancelot, convinces Dave, passing himself off as Guinevere, that I will speak to the king on his behalf. Even a bonehead like Dave will be able to see that makes more sense.

OSBERT. It's a great plan.

EDGAR. It's our *only* plan.

Instrumental music. They both exit.

Scene Seventeen – The Farce

GUINEVERE *enters from the other side with a clipboard, writing lyrics. (NB. Even though the actual* GUINEVERE *and* DAVE'*s impression of Guinevere are played by the same actor, actual* GUINEVERE *is distinguishable to us because she has a better costume and wig and carries herself as a woman rather than a man in a dress.)*

GUINEVERE *is composing song lyrics. They are exactly the same as the opening lyrics to 'Milkshake' by Kelis, only she replaces the word 'boys' with the word 'squires'.*

EDGAR *enters in Lancelot disguise, holding his wig.*

EDGAR. Where is that idiot, Dave? Where are you? Oh no, it's Guinevere. I don't want that.

He puts the wig on and is about to exit when she sees him. Real GUINEVERE *likes* LANCELOT. *A lot.*

GUINEVERE. Lancelot! What a lovely surprise. What brings you here?

EDGAR (*as Lancelot*). I was just out… looking at things. But you're probably off to see the king, so I won't hold you up.

GUINEVERE. Wait! I'm actually on my way to the lake. It's so... hot. I was going to cool off.

Seductive jazz music starts as she slowly makes her way down towards EDGAR.

EDGAR (*as Lancelot*). Before seeing the king?

GUINEVERE. I don't have any particular plans. How about you?

EDGAR (*as Lancelot*). No, no particular plans but –

GUINEVERE. Then we are free agents in this... sticky heat.

EDGAR (*as Lancelot*). But do you not have a message for the king?

GUINEVERE. Do I? Tell me what you'd like me to tell him and I'll do it for you. Or perhaps it would be best coming from you?

EDGAR (*as Lancelot*). Something so... important... should come from you, no?

GUINEVERE. So you feel the same way?

EDGAR (*as Lancelot*). Yes. About what?

GUINEVERE. Let's stop pretending.

EDGAR (*as Lancelot*). I agree. About what exactly?

GUINEVERE. Kiss me.

EDGAR (*as Lancelot*). Sorry?

GUINEVERE *grabs* EDGAR *and kisses him passionately.*

That was... amazing.

GUINEVERE. I'll tell him now.

EDGAR (*as Lancelot*). About cancelling the squires' show?

GUINEVERE. What squires? No. About our burgeoning love for one another.

EDGAR (*as Lancelot*). No, don't do that!

GUINEVERE. But we must. Remember, there are no lies in Camelot.

EDGAR (*as Lancelot*). But, madame!

GUINEVERE. We're in too deep now, Lancelot. Adieu.

She exits. Instrumental music.

EDGAR. What the fu…

OSBERT *enters.*

OSBERT. Did you find Dave?

EDGAR. No, but I found Guinevere.

OSBERT. On her way to the king?

EDGAR. Yes. Except…

OSBERT. What?

EDGAR. Do you want the good news or the bad news?

OSBERT. The good?

EDGAR. The good news is that it wasn't Dave I just snogged.

OSBERT. What?! You snogged Guinevere?!

EDGAR. I didn't have any choice! She's clearly crazy about Lancelot and is now off to tell the king about it.

OSBERT. But what about telling him to cancel our show?

EDGAR. Exactly. We have to get her back on track!

OSBERT. How?

EDGAR. Got it. Give me your impression of King Arthur.

OSBERT (*as Arthur*). 'Tell me a joke. No, entertain me.'

EDGAR. Wow, that's uncanny.

OSBERT. Thanks.

EDGAR. Right. Put on this costume.

EDGAR *starts dressing* OSBERT *as Arthur.*

Right. You, disguised as the king, intercept Guinevere, tell her you're open to three-way relationships and then make a quick exit.

OSBERT. Could that work?

EDGAR. It's the next logical step. And as fortune would have it, Guinevere is coming back. Quick. I'll hide.

EDGAR hides. DAVE enters as Guinevere and sees OSBERT dressed up and takes him to be the real ARTHUR. (NB. OSBERT and ARTHUR are played by the same actor.) So in this section, they both believe the other to be the genuine article.

DAVE (*to himself*). King Arthur?! Sweet. Well, here goes.

OSBERT (*as Arthur*). Darling, I've missed you so much!

DAVE (*as Guinevere*). Arthur, my love, I have something to tell you.

OSBERT (*as Arthur*). Me too. I think we should have an open relationship.

DAVE (*as Guinevere*). Really?

OSBERT (*as Arthur*). Yes, so if you happen to have smooched anyone else, say in the last three minutes, all is forgiven, as long as we never speak of it again. And let us seal this pact with a kiss!

They kiss.

My goodness, you are a good kisser.

DAVE (*as Guinevere*). So are you. But I have to tell you something too!

OSBERT (*as Arthur*). No, don't tell me, tell the actual king. I mean, tell me back at court. Bye.

He quickly exits.

DAVE (*as Guinevere*). Arthur, come back! You must cancel… (*As himself.*) Damn. So close!

French-café music starts.

Oh crap. It's Lancelot!

DAVE attempts to hide. The real LANCELOT enters. (NB. EDGAR as fake Lancelot and the real LANCELOT are played by the same actor.)

LANCELOT (*aside*). Zut alors, it's Guinevere. I must crush these rumours I've heard about us getting orf togezzer. Guinevere?

DAVE (*as Guinevere; forced to stand*). Lancelot. How are you?

LANCELOT. Not so good. 'Ave you 'eard ze rumours about uz getting orf togezzer?

DAVE (*as Guinevere*). You got off with Guinevere?! I mean me?

LANCELOT. No! But there are rumours we did. And when I find who is responsible, I will barbecue zer faces!

DAVE (*as Guinevere*). Good for you.

LANCELOT. But just to check. You 'ave no desire to kiss me?

DAVE (*as Guinevere*). Not right now.

LANCELOT. Perhaps if circumstances were different for uz both?

He swings towards DAVE *as Guinevere, who ducks, and so* LANCELOT *smashes face-first into the wall.*

DAVE (*as Guinevere*). I can't really answer for Guinevere. I mean myself. But I'm afraid I have to urgently get to court.

LANCELOT. Very well, my horse is in this stable. Allow me to ride you!

DAVE (*as Guinevere*). Yes. That is something that I would do…

They enter the stable and we hear the horse exit. Enter OSBERT.

OSBERT. I can't believe that just happened. I've got to tell Edgar. He'll never believe it. I just kissed the queen! I knew I was destined for greatness. Edgar? Where are you? Edgar, mate! Edgar?!

He searches the stage until EDGAR *enters.*

What happened, did you get Guinevere back on track?

EDGAR. I didn't get a chance. Lancelot arrived and they rode off on his horse. Hang on, what's this? (*Picks up a Spanish cookbook.*) A Spanish cookbook? Why would Guinevere be carrying a Spanish cookbook? Oh God, that means *that* was Dave *impersonating* Guinevere!

OSBERT. Oh God. That means Lancelot is taking Dave to see the king now, dressed as Guinevere! We have to stop him!

EDGAR. Osbert, to court!

He exits. A fanfare as the location changes to the castle. DAVE *enters (dressed as Guinevere). We're at court.*

DAVE *(to himself)*. Right, here we go – second attempt. You've tricked the king once you can do it again. *And* you've tricked Lancelot. You're a flipping natural, Dave. Just remember – you're Guinevere, Guinevere – (*Guinevere impression.*) 'Guinevere!'

Real ARTHUR *enters. Another fanfare.*

ARTHUR. Dave! In a wig and dress! Totes jokes. How's the play coming along?

DAVE, *although perplexed, has no choice but to accept that* ARTHUR *has seen through his disguise, and must simply be* DAVE.

DAVE. Yeah, not bad actually.

ARTHUR. This is one of the costumes, is it?

DAVE. Yes. Actually.

ARTHUR. Who are you supposed to be?

DAVE. Like… Guinevere.

ARTHUR. Guinevere?

DAVE. Yes.

ARTHUR. Guinevere?!

DAVE. Right.

ARTHUR. Wa-hey!

He mimes running his hands over her body. DAVE *returns the 'compliment'.*

Hey! What do you think you're doing?! I'm the king.

French-café music signals that LANCELOT *approaches.*

Ah, Lancelot!

DAVE (*aside*). Oh crap. This won't end well.

He starts to remove the Guinevere wig.

ARTHUR. No, no, leave it on. I want to see whether you can convince him.

DAVE. No, please.

ARTHUR. I SAID leave it on!!

DAVE *has no choice.* LANCELOT *enters. He's still convinced by* DAVE*'s disguise.*

LANCELOT. My Lord. Madame Guinevere.

DAVE (*as Guinevere*). Lancelot. Back so soon?

ARTHUR *can hardly contain his amusement.*

LANCELOT. Yes, I 'ave come back because I wanted to assure you that I will get to the bottom of whoever is wandering about disguised as you.

ARTHUR. This is a terrible thing you speak of, Lancelot. Someone doing an impression of my Guinevere?!

LANCELOT. Oui, My Lord.

ARTHUR. And people believing it's actually her?

LANCELOT. Hard to believe, but oui.

ARTHUR. But they'd have to be quite gullible, don't you think?

LANCELOT. Never underestimate how stupid some people can be.

ARTHUR. *How* stupid would you say?

LANCELOT. If you're asking me how stupid someone would 'ave to be not to recognise an imposter standing right in front of their face? I'd 'ave to say monumentally doopey. Catastrophically goofy!

ARTHUR. Don't you think that's funny, my love?

DAVE (*as Guinevere*). Yes. Ha, ha, ha!

ARTHUR. Well, Lancelot, you'd better ride off on your horse and root out the imposter.

LANCELOT. Mark my words, I will find zem! (*Kisses* DAVE *as Guinevere's hand.*) Au revoir!

He exits. ARTHUR *can no longer contain himself.*

ARTHUR. Oh my God, Dave, that is seriously the best laugh I've had in ages. Such bants! And listen, really good luck with the show tomorrow.

DAVE. Tomorrow?!

ARTHUR. And I really hope I don't have to kill you because… You. Are. Hilarious!

He leaves and reappears.

HILARIOUS! Show time in a couple of hours!

DAVE. Hours?! What is happening with time?!

Instrumental music. ARTHUR *exits.*

Scene Eighteen – Creating the Stories

DAVE *is removing the Guinevere costume.* OSBERT *and* EDGAR *are sat looking gloomy.*

EDGAR. Unbelievable! So now to add to our problems, we have Lancelot on the warpath.

DAVE. He'll never work out it was you pretending to be him.

EDGAR. Unless the king reveals we've been dressing up.

DAVE. He'll be more focused on Guinevere seeking an open relationship.

OSBERT. No. Because she thinks he's already given her permission for it.

EDGAR. No. Because that was a conversation between you two before you got off together!

ACT ONE, SCENE EIGHTEEN 53

DAVE. Oh yeah.

EDGAR. So. In the best-case scenario, in approximately one hour's time, we're scheduled to present the stories of Camelot to the world or face death. Which could be workable except we still have no stories!

DAVE. Although the characters of Camelot are pretty interesting. More than interesting.

OSBERT. Hang on, hang on. You might be on to something there.

DAVE. Normally am.

OSBERT. What if we took these 'interesting people', and we made them *more* interesting?

EDGAR. You mean make stuff up?!

DAVE (*gasps*). Nooooooo.

EDGAR. Osbert, that is crackers mental. Lying?!

OSBERT. We won't lie, we'll… embellish.

DAVE. What, like on a burger?

 EDGAR *punches him.*

OSBERT. Remember. The final chapter of *The Acting Bible* – Dramatisation and Embellishment.

 A collective moment of realisation.

EDGAR. Could that work?

OSBERT. Yes.

EDGAR. Could we take the seemingly useless strands of what we know about Camelot –

OSBERT. One hundred per cent.

EDGAR. – and spin them into stories –

OSBERT. Yeah I just said that.

EDGAR. – that could survive the test of time –

OSBERT. Literally in the book.

EDGAR. – and still be told thousands of years from now?

OSBERT. Not stories, my friend…

ALL. Legends.

They all air-grab dramatically.

EDGAR. Did you just do the wrong arm?

DAVE. No.

EDGAR. Let's make a show!

DAVE (*tries again on his own*). Legends.

Scene Nineteen – 'Making the Show' Montage

Montage begins. The action is choreographed to the following sections that are announced in voice-over.

VOICE. Script writing.

Busy mime-writing.

Set and costume.

Busy at work.

Devising.

Green Knight presentation.

Character development.

Merlin presentation.

Directing.

'Sword in the Stone' idea.

Choreography.

Series of stupid lifts.

As the montage comes to its finale…

ACT ONE, SCENE NINETEEN

LANCELOT (*off*). Where is he?!

Music abruptly cuts.

I will find you and eat you, Roast-Beef Boy.

EDGAR *looks into the wings.*

EDGAR. Oh no. It's Lancelot! He's got his wooden spatula with the split down the middle. He'll split me in two because I dressed up as him and kissed Guinevere! What do we do?

DAVE. Here. Put this bag on your head.

Instrumental music. DAVE *forces a large hessian bag over* EDGAR*'s head. The bag reaches his knees.*

EDGAR. How does this help?

OSBERT. It won't. We have to hide him somewhere.

DAVE. Quick, I'll hide him in here.

DAVE *forces* EDGAR *behind the stable door.* EDGAR *runs off* (*to become* LANCELOT). SM *switch to take* EDGAR*'s place behind the door* (*in an identical hessian bag*).

EDGAR (*on mic offstage*). Isn't this the first place he'll look?

'Edgar' (*but it's actually the* SM *in the bag*) *pushes open the top stable door.*

DAVE. Well it will be if you don't shut up!

EDGAR (*on mic offstage*). I'm not staying here.

SM *as Edgar walks onstage.* (*Stable doors are left open.*) OSBERT *is by the trapdoor.*

OSBERT. Hide him in here!

DAVE *escorts* SM *as Edgar to the trapdoor.*

DAVE. Get in there! Just get in.

SM *as Edgar steps into the trapdoor.* DAVE *and* OSBERT *try to block/hide the trapdoor.* LANCELOT *enters from the corridor.*

LANCELOT. Where is he?! Where are you hiding him?!

He searches then heads up a ladder. Meanwhile SM *as Edgar has exited under the stage through the trapdoor.* LANCELOT *heads to* DAVE *and* OSBERT.

Out of my way! A-ha! A trapdoor. You will not escape me, Roast-Beef Boy!

He heads down into the trapdoor.

OSBERT. Damn, what do we do now?

DAVE. I've got an idea. Grab another sack. We just need a decoy.

He grabs a full-sized dummy.

Put the sack on the dummy. Quick!

OSBERT *does this.* SM *as Edgar appears at the upstage double doors in a sack.*

EDGAR (*on mic offstage*). This isn't working, guys!

DAVE. It's okay, we've got a decoy!

DAVE *pushes* SM *as Edgar back behind the doors.* LANCELOT *appears in the trapdoor and sees the dummy.*

LANCELOT. A-ha!

DAVE *grabs the dummy from* OSBERT.

DAVE. No, you won't take our friend.

He puts the dummy over his shoulder and runs into the stable. LANCELOT *follows in pursuit.*

LANCELOT. Come here!

OSBERT *closes the stable door.* SM *as Edgar appears again at the upstage double doors.*

EDGAR (*on mic offstage*). Where is he?

OSBERT. Get back in there, Edgar!

OSBERT *runs to* SM *as Edgar to push him back through the doors. Then closes the trapdoor.* DAVE *enters from the corridor with the dummy and collides with* OSBERT. OSBERT *takes the dummy.*

LANCELOT (*off*). Where is he?!

DAVE looks into the wings just as SM *as Edgar appears again through the double doors.* DAVE *turns and grabs him* (*although he thinks it's the dummy*) *and leads down the stage stairs.* LANCELOT *enters from the corridor.*

DAVE (*feigning horror*). No. Don't take our friend!

OSBERT. No, Dave. No! That's actually –

LANCELOT. Too late. The game is up!

LANCELOT throws SM *as Edgar over his shoulder.*

(*On exit.*) To the dungeon with you! You will never perform your show now!

DAVE (*laughing with relief*). Imagine his face when he finds out he has the dummy!

OSBERT takes the sack off the dummy and throws the dummy at DAVE.

DAVE. Edgar, no! What's happened to you, mate?!

OSBERT. That's the dummy, you dummy!

DAVE. So where's Edgar? (*Beat.*) Oh, I see what I've done there.

VOICE. Your Royal Highnesses, lords, ladies, dignitaries, people of Camelot. Welcome to ArthurFest. Please take your seats. Our headline act will be commencing shortly: *The Legends of King Arthur*!

OSBERT. No! We can't do the show with just the two of us! What are we going to do?

Big dramatic cliffhanger SFX. Lights fade on a very concerned DAVE *and* OSBERT *holding the dummy between them.*

End of Act One.

ACT TWO

Scene Twenty – Opening Number

EDGAR *is locked in a dungeon in chains. His intro music begins.*

EDGAR *(singing)*.
In this jail cell
Chained up on the floor
All my tomorrows
Just blown out the door
Why, oh why
Will anybody know what I was doing this for?

EDGAR *rips open his shirt, revealing his bare chest. Overly dramatic.*

I'm not a hero
I'm just a useless squire
A feeble actor
Lacking all desire
Light the fire
Will anybody know what we were trying for?

DAVE *and* OSBERT *appear in spotlights.*

DAVE/OSBERT *(singing)*.
The show must continue

EDGAR *(singing)*.
Free of copyright

DAVE/OSBERT *(singing)*.
The show must continue

EDGAR *(singing)*.
We'll give the lawyers a fright

DAVE/OSBERT *(singing)*.
Out of this prison we'll be breaking
You out and we can go and do our show

OSBERT (*singing*).
> And your smile will return
> Come on, let's do this
> We're against the clock

DAVE (*singing*).
> We'll use an explosive
> And we'll blow the lock

EDGAR (*singing*).
> The festival fires are burning
> But inside this cell I'm yearning to be free

Big explosion. EDGAR *has broken out of his chains.*

> The show must continue

DAVE/OSBERT (*singing*).
> The show must continue

EDGAR (*singing*).
> Please don't pull the plug

DAVE/OSBERT (*singing*).
> The show must continue

EDGAR (*singing*).
> Must continue

DAVE (*singing*).
> Or we'll be out of luck

EDGAR (*singing*).
> Out of this prison cell I'm breaking

OSBERT (*singing*).
> The stage it is awaiting for our show

ALL (*singing*).
> We must go on!

EDGAR. Yes!! Dave! (*Chest-bump.*) Osbert!

> OSBERT *jumps out of the way so* OSBERT *misses the chest-bump.*

OSBERT. Right, let's do this – set the stage! Announcer, let them know we'll be on stage shortly!

The squires construct a performance tent during the following.

ANNOUNCER (*voice-over*). Welcome to this evening's performance of *The Legends of King Arthur.* Please take your seats, the show is about to begin.

Upbeat underscore music – 'The Floral Dance'.

Scene Twenty-One – How Arthur Became King

OSBERT *and* EDGAR *enter and address the ArthurFest audience. They're nervous actors.*

OSBERT. Thank you! Your Majesty. Good people of Camelot and beyond. If we do not offend, it is not with our goodwill that you think we come not to offend. But with goodwill.

EDGAR. We are not offensive. We will perform for you the untold tales of Arthur's great knights, which through their own might will become legendary.

OSBERT. They tell thus far untold tales of great gallantry, chivalry and honour.

EDGAR. We are not a cast of one hundred.

OSBERT. We are but three.

EDGAR. Yet we will play a cast of one hundred.

OSBERT. Pray tell, Edgar. How?

EDGAR. Through the theatrical device known as 'multi-roling'.

OSBERT. We begin with the true untold story of how King Arthur became –

EDGAR. A legend –

OSBERT *kicks him*.

King. I meant to say king.

Song begins. Musical rock-story style with full action. MERLIN *enters in full* MERLIN *attire.*

MERLIN (*singing*).
Who am I? I'm an enigma
I'm almost impossible to explain
I experience all events looking forwards in reverse
Which means I know the fate that's sealed, for the universe

They call me Merlin, yeah they do
And I've got a story just for you
It's about a boy that I once knew
In fact I still know him and you do too

ARTHUR *enters and the rock-metal verse kicks in.* EDGAR *supports the story with action.*

It's Arthur, what a 'king legend
The one true king, so savvy and bright
It's Arthur, what a 'king legend
You tell him a tale, he'll make you a knight

But let's begin at the beginning, with Arthur's succession
When the stars all aligned to grant him possession
Of a sword that distinguished him, distinct from the rest
But from where to extract it? What would be best?

Could it be from the jaws of a fire-breathing dragon?
Could it be from a rip in the sky? No!
Could it be from the centre of the Earth or perhaps
From the gap in a baby's cry? Huh?
Could it be from the sphincter of an angry woodland beast?
Could it be from an ice-cream cone?
No it had to be more simple and it couldn't be surreal
It had to come from a stone

EDGAR *is now under a grey cloth with the sword poking out.* ARTHUR *pulls the sword from the stone and wields it over a guitar solo.* MERLIN *places a gold cardboard crown on* ARTHUR's *head during this.*

On his first day as king, Arthur wandered through the woods
He was trying to make sense of this gig
When he met a crazy man who was as tall as a house
And on the hunt for a mythical pig

They started to converse but they soon fell out
And in order to settle the score

They both drew swords but what Arthur didn't know
Was that this was Pellinore!

Stop!

Arthur, what are you doing?
This man is as fearsome as they come
You don't want to die on your first day in the job
That would be kinda dumb

ARTHUR. But –

MERLIN (*singing*).
Don't speak, don't say a word
For that would be a mistake
I have a friend that I want you to meet
Her name is Viv and she lives in a lake

ARTHUR *follows* MERLIN *to the lake.*

Viv, are you there, my love?
Reveal yourself if you would
Arthur is here and he needs a new sword
Cos the one he's got is no good

VIVIANE *rises out of the lake and sings.*

VIVIANE (*singing*).
My name is Viv and I live in a lake
And I have a rare gift for you
It's a sword called Excalibur and it's got magic powers
And a special sheath too
Which do you think will protect you the best?
Give me your answer in song

ARTHUR (*singing*).
Is it the sword?

VIVIANE (*singing*).
No, I thought you'd say that
But I'm afraid that you're wrong

VIVIANE *disappears.*

MERLIN (*spoken*). The sheath represents peace, Arthur. Although you can kill anything you want at any time, you should always strive for armistice. It's something of a paradox I grant you, but give it a go. Return to your fight with Pellinore.

MERLIN *exits,* PELLINORE *appears.* ARTHUR *now wields Excalibur.*

PELLINORE *and* ARTHUR *fight.*

PELLINORE (*singing*).
This kid is good, what's happening?
He's getting the better of me
His prowess with the sword is really super-clear
I've ended up down on one knee

(*Spoken.*) Go ahead and strike your blow.

ARTHUR. No.

PELLINORE. What do you mean 'No'?

ARTHUR (*singing*).
You have strength and courage when you fight
I'm going to make you a... knight

BOTH (*singing*).
The First Knight of the Round Table
The first knight to make the grade
The legacy of Arthur begins
With a sword and an awesome upgrade.

They bow, high-five and exit.

Scene Twenty-Two – Morgana

MORGANA *appears.*

MORGANA (*as Dave*). Meanwhile, Morgana le Fay has something to say...

Instrumental music begins.

(*As* MORGANA.) No! I am the eldest child of Uther Pendragon. The throne is rightfully mine. Just because he's a man!! Fine, if you smite me then I shall smite you back. With bells on! My boy Mordred's ascension to the throne will be 'sped up'. And the wannabe knights will fall by the wayside in my scheme to... make them fall by the wayside.

Laughing, she exits.

Scene Twenty-Three – Sir Gawain and the Green Knight

OSBERT, *dressed as* GAWAIN, *is pushing* EDGAR, *half-dressed as* ARTHUR, *on to the stage.*

EDGAR (*sotto*). They won't get it!

OSBERT (*sotto*). It's the same costume. Just go! (*To audience.*) Your Majesty, people of Camelot, the role of King Arthur will now be passed to a second actor. Why, you ask?

EDGAR. Because there's only three of –

OSBERT *places his hand over* EDGAR*'s mouth.*

OSBERT. Because a man of such great stature, as our noble king, embodies two men!

EDGAR. That is what I meant.

OSBERT *hands the crown to* EDGAR, *moves to his position and kneels.*

They begin acting. Or their best attempt to get it right (think: Rude Mechanicals). We're in Arthur's court.

GAWAIN. Your Majesty.

He stands.

ARTHUR. Rise.

GAWAIN *kneels then rises again.*

And who are you, Gawain?

GAWAIN. Gawain.

ARTHUR. I mean, who are you?

GAWAIN. Gawain.

ARTHUR. A servant?

GAWAIN. Who hopes to one day become a knight. Everybody thinks you're amazing.

ARTHUR. And what do people think of me? I mean, thank you.

GAWAIN. You're amazing.

ARTHUR. Thank you. But I must show beyond doubt that Camelot is the greatest court in the world.

GAWAIN. Indeed.

ARTHUR. You mean how? Well, Gawain, I will populate Camelot with knights of astounding valour and courage. Their escapades will become the stuff of legends.

GAWAIN. And how will you find such said knights?

GAWAIN *trips on his way up the steps.*

Them. Such said them knights. Where are the knights?

ARTHUR. I will embark on a journey and seek them out.

GAWAIN. Inspired. But to assure your legacy endures for centuries to come, surely these stories of Camelot will need to be comparable to no other story. Like… *my* story.

ARTHUR. You have a story, Gawain? Then let us hear it. And if it's worthy then I will appoint you Sir Gawain.

EDGAR. And now begins 'The Legend of Gawain and the Green Knight'!

SFX: 'The Legend of Gawain and the Green Knight' jingle.

OSBERT. Once upon a time. Well, last New Year's Eve in fact…

EDGAR. Longer ago, surely?

OSBERT. Many New Year's Eves ago surely, Gawain was at this party…

The party begins. EDGAR *becomes a friend –* NOBBY. *Medieval party music. They dance awkwardly.*

NOBBY. Great New Year's Eve party, Gawain.

GAWAIN. Yeah.

NOBBY. Have you seen that massive weird guy who's just rocked up?

GAWAIN. We're all a bit weird, Nobby?

NOBBY. Yeah but he's green. And so is his horse. Which he's riding around the kitchen.

Peril music. The GREEN KNIGHT *appears with an axe.*

GREEN KNIGHT. Right, you bunch of scaredy-cats, who's up for a game?

GAWAIN. Who are you calling a scaredy-cat!

GREEN KNIGHT. You!

GAWAIN. Right!

Starts heading towards the GREEN KNIGHT.

GREEN KNIGHT. Wait! Here are the rules of the game: You get to strike me a single blow, anywhere you fancy, with this axe. And then, within a year and a day, I get to strike you back. What d'you reckon?

NOBBY. I reckon that sounds mental.

GAWAIN (*grabbing the axe*). Right. Out the back. Don't want to make a mess in here.

GREEN KNIGHT. You're the boss.

They exit. There's a chop. GAWAIN *returns.*

GAWAIN. Sorted. Chopped his noggin off.

NOBBY. Right. Good. (*Pause.*) Quite a short game really.

GAWAIN. Yep.

NOBBY. Do you think that's what he was expecting?

GAWAIN. Who knows, Nobby? Who knows?

GREEN KNIGHT. Arrghhhh!

Chilling music. The GREEN KNIGHT *appears, with his head own under his arm.* SM *is part of this costume.*

GAWAIN. Lord have mercy! What sorcery is this?

ACT TWO, SCENE TWENTY-THREE 67

GREEN KNIGHT. You will find me in the Green Chapel in the Forest of the Wirral. Come to me in a year and a day and you'll get what you deserve!

The GREEN KNIGHT *exits.*

NOBBY. Makes more sense now. As a game I mean.

GAWAIN. Nobby, I'm gonna die!

NOBBY. Unless you can do that with your head. Can you?

GAWAIN. No.

NOBBY *exits.*

And so before the year was up I went in search of the Forest of the Wirral.

Fast music. He starts to ride an imaginary horse on the spot. Music abruptly stops. He dismounts.

It was Christmas Eve –

He realises he's not in the light and moves.

By Christmas Eve, I was tired, hungry and lost.

BERTILAK *appears from nowhere.*

Ah, excuse me. I'm lost.

BERTILAK. I see. Very well, you may stay in my castle. Three nights tops and it's lights-out at eleven.

GAWAIN. That's very accommodating of you but I need to reach the Green Chapel in the Forest of the Wirral before the year is out.

'Green Chapel – 1 Mile' sign appears.

Oh and that's very convenient. Great!

BERTILAK. I'm Sir Baz Bertilak and the wife will be even happier.

GAWAIN. Is your castle far away?

BERTILAK. Nope.

BERTILAK *turns and opens a set of invisible doors with a creak and enters his castle.*

Well come on then, if you're coming.

GAWAIN. Bit weird.

GAWAIN *follows and the atmosphere changes. He turns to close the doors.*

BERTILAK. Leave the doors, they don't exist.

A dog snarls and barks. BERTILAK *kicks the dog.*

And neither does that. But she does.

MRS BERTILAK *appears. George Gershwin's 'Rhapsody in Blue' kicks in.*

MRS BERTILAK. Hello. And who do we have here?

BERTILAK. He's come for a rendezvous with the Green Knight but needs to rest up first.

GAWAIN. How did you know that?!

BERTILAK. It's the talk of the forest, old chap. Now, here's the way things work around here. I go off hunting right now and while I'm away, the wife tries to seduce you. (*To* MRS BERTILAK.) What do you do?

MRS BERTILAK. I try to seduce him, darling.

BERTILAK (*to* GAWAIN). And what do you do?

GAWAIN. I wouldn't do anything like that.

BERTILAK. Why, what are you saying about my wife?

GAWAIN. No. I mean she's really nice but –

BERTILAK. I'm messing with you! But she will try it on. So what do you do?

GAWAIN. Resist?

BERTILAK. If you can! And then when I return from hunting, I'll give you whatever I've won from the land and in return, you'll give me whatever you've won.

GAWAIN. Won?

BERTILAK. Off've her. Whatever I 'win' I give to you and whatever you 'win' you give to me. Gettit?

GAWAIN. I think so.

BERTILAK. Well I'm glad someone does! Right then, time for lights-out. And time for me to go a-hunting. Night night and see you in the morning, boy-o!

He exits

MRS BERTILAK. Here's a hot flannel.

The lights dim.

Let me tuck you in.

A bed appears (accompanied by another burst of 'Rhapsody in Blue'), which they stand behind.

My flaming loins! How can we possibly cool them down?

GAWAIN. Got any board games?

MRS BERTILAK. Kiss me!

GAWAIN. Kerplunk?

MRS BERTILAK. Steal me away! Take me deep into the woods and –

GAWAIN. Look, I'm sorry but I'm really not comfortable with any of this.

SFX: record scratch. The atmospheric lighting returns.

MRS BERTILAK. Okay, fine. The truth is, neither am I. If I'm honest I'm well tired and I thought you'd be easier. It's just part of the test

GAWAIN. Test?!

MRS BERTILAK. Nothing! Just give me a peck on the cheek. Do it! Before he returns!

GAWAIN *kisses her – kissing SFX.*

And take this piece of green ribbon with a bell on it. It could help you tomorrow with the Green Knight.

GAWAIN. Does it have magical powers?

MRS BERTILAK. Does it heck. But I wouldn't mention it to my husband. Night then.

Lights down and lights up. SFX: cockerel. BERTILAK (*now in bed*) *has swapped places with* MRS BERTILAK, *who is now stood beside the bed.*

BERTILAK. Right, let's get this over with. This is as awkward for me as it is for you, lad, but I don't make the rules.

MRS BERTILAK. You do actually.

BERTILAK. That's true, I do! So what have you got for me? Cos there's a wild boar out there with your name on it.

GAWAIN *kisses him briefly on the cheek. Kissing SFX.*

Is that it?!

GAWAIN. Yep.

BERTILAK. Do you still want the wild boar?

GAWAIN. Not really.

BERTILAK. Right. I'll let it loose then. Can I just say that you're possibly the most boring guest we've ever hosted.

MRS BERTILAK. I had to Kerplunk myself silly.

BERTILAK. But I'll forgive you. As you're about to die tomorrow! Good luck with the Green Knight, lad.

GAWAIN. Wow.

DAVE *and* EDGAR *slide offstage with the bed.* GAWAIN *is alone in the forest. Spooky music.*

Ah the Green Chapel at last. I'm here, ready to receive my blow.

GREEN KNIGHT (*off*). Is that you, Gawain?

GAWAIN. Yes. I've come to honour our agreement and prove my courage.

GREEN KNIGHT (*off*). Good man. Just sharpening my axe.

Sharpening SFX. The GREEN KNIGHT *enters.*

Feeling scared?

GAWAIN. Certainly not.

GREEN KNIGHT. Bit of a tough guy, are we?

GAWAIN. Can we just get on with it please?

ACT TWO, SCENE TWENTY-THREE

GREEN KNIGHT. I thought I'd take my blow in the same place you took your blow if that's okay? So assume the position.

GAWAIN. On my knees?

GREEN KNIGHT. Normally is.

He raises his axe above his head and then pauses.

Did you have a nice Christmas?

GAWAIN. Not really, no.

GREEN KNIGHT. Can be a tricky time of year, can't it. Family issues?

GAWAIN. Can we just get on with it please!

GREEN KNIGHT. Alright, keep your hair on.

He swings his axe around his head, dramatically and elaborately, infuriating GAWAIN. *Then brings it to the ground, missing* GAWAIN.

GAWAIN. What are you doing?!

GREEN KNIGHT. You flinched!

GAWAIN. I didn't flinch!

GREEN KNIGHT. You did too.

GAWAIN. Oh for goodness' sake. You are possibly the most infuriating person in the world!

GREEN KNIGHT. And you're the flinchiest.

GAWAIN. Will you get on with it before I do it myself!

The GREEN KNIGHT *swings his axe again, brings it down, and at the last minute veers it away to the ground beside him.* GAWAIN *reaches up to his neck and presses a nick where the blade has cut him. He leaps to his feet.*

A-ha! You nicked me! That's it, you've taken your blow, I am an honest man and have honoured the rules of the game. So, if you blow me again, I shall defend myself!

The GREEN KNIGHT *starts to laugh.*

GREEN KNIGHT. But you're not honest, are you, Gawain?

GAWAIN. Excuse me?

GREEN KNIGHT. You lied to me.

GAWAIN. How have I lied?

GREEN KNIGHT. Because you didn't tell me about the green ribbon with the bell on it that my wife gave you, did you?!

GAWAIN. Your wife?!

The GREEN KNIGHT *removes his mask and cape (or whatever) to reveal himself as* BERTILAK.

Bertilak?!

BERTILAK. Didn't see that coming, did you, lad?

GAWAIN. What's going on?!

BERTILAK. You have proven yourself to be a brave and noble man, Gawain. You're free to go.

He turns to depart.

GAWAIN. Why in the name of sanity would you wish to test that?!

BERTILAK. Okay, cards on the table, it wasn't my idea. This whole thing was an assignment.

GAWAIN. From who?!

BERTILAK. My lips are sealed.

GAWAIN *draws his sword.*

GAWAIN. Tell me.

BERTILAK. I can say what it rhymes with.

GAWAIN. Well?

BERTILAK. Morgana le Fay. Oh crap, that's actually it.

GAWAIN. Morgana le Fay?

BERTILAK. Gotta run!

BERTILAK *exits.* ARTHUR (EDGAR) *enters.*

ARTHUR. Gawain.

GAWAIN. Sire!

ARTHUR. Morgana le Fay you say?!

GAWAIN. I do say, Morgana le Fay.

ARTHUR. My sister?! More likely half-sister. What's her game?

GAWAIN. I believe there's more to her than meets the eye, my king.

ARTHUR. It would seem so, Gawain, it would seem so. But to more pressing matters – I have no doubt that your remarkable story will become legendary. Everyone across the land will hear 'The Tale of Gawain and the Green Knight'.

SFX: 'The Legend of Gawain and the Green Knight' jingle.

Arise, Sir Gawain.

GAWAIN *kneels.* ARTHUR *realises he's forgotten to knight him so goes to knight him with his sword. Except* GAWAIN *thinks they're skipping it and stands, so* ARTHUR *accidentally bonks him on the head on the way up.* GAWAIN *stumbles away, nursing his head.*

And now I must seek more legendary tales like yours, Gawain.

He exits.

Scene Twenty-Four – Sir Percival and the Black Knight

MORGANA *appears, still furious.*

MORGANA. Damn Bertilak. He was supposed to kill Gawain. Yet he was seduced by 'honesty' and 'nobility'... euch! Yuck! But I won't let such trifles stand in my way. Continue on your quest, Arthur, but I will be there to thwart you! At every stage you will be... thwarted! Thwarty thwarty thwart thwart!

ARTHUR *passes a Dutchman –* PERCIVAL *– looking troubled (in a Rodin's* The Thinker *pose), sat on a three-legged stool.*

ARTHUR. Whoa! My good man, you appear troubled and vexed.

PERCIVAL. I am troubled. And I am vexed.

ARTHUR. Ah well, moving on. I'm seeking men who have stories of exhibiting great courage, chivalry and/or valour. Perhaps you know someone?

PERCIVAL. I do indeed. A great man; incredibly strong, incredibly brave, a man who eats chivalry for breakfast.

ARTHUR. Who is this almighty being?

PERCIVAL. 'Tis I. Percival.

ARTHUR. And yet you complain of trouble and vexation.

PERCIVAL. Because I was forsaken by a woman.

ARTHUR. A woman forsooked you?!

PERCIVAL. A beautiful damsel.

ARTHUR. In distress?

PERCIVAL. No, she was wearing her own clothes.

ARTHUR. Percival, please tell me your story, for this must be *some* woman.

PERCIVAL. Very well. It involves me – and the Black Knight.

SFX: 'The Legend of Percival and the Black Knight' jingle, then we hear the winds of Avalon.

I heard her before I saw her. I was riding through the Vale of Avalon and her cries echoed up through the valley.

ARTHUR. You mean like… sobbing.

PERCIVAL. Far from it. She was furious. She was being pursued by the Black Knight.

GUINEVERE *enters.*

GUINEVERE. Come on then, where are you?! Where have you got to?

She scans the horizon.

PERCIVAL. Hey, baby.

She turns. Slowly.

GUINEVERE. Who are you and what do you want?

PERCIVAL. My name is Percival and I'm here to help.

ACT TWO, SCENE TWENTY-FOUR

GUINEVERE. Oh really? And how do you think you might 'help' me, Percy?

PERCIVAL. Percival actually. I will protect you from the man that's vexed you.

GUINEVERE. So, you're prepared to just wade in there, without any real context and just start fighting?

PERCIVAL. Pretty much.

GUINEVERE. Have you ever considered the fact that that kind of machismo-driven logic might actually be quite idiotic, Perky?

PERCIVAL. It's Percy. I mean Percival! Wait, what?

Drone/drumming/something approaches.

GUINEVERE. He's back.

PERCIVAL *draws his sword, looking out over audience.*

Take one more step and I'll serve you up your own perky, Percy.

PERCIVAL *sees what's approaching. He backs up, scared.*

PERCIVAL. The Black Knight! Riding on the back of a lion!

The BLACK KNIGHT *enters on the other side of the stage, riding an ostrich.*

BLACK KNIGHT. Over here!

PERCIVAL. The Black Knight! Riding on the back of a...?! Where is your lion, Black Knight?

BLACK KNIGHT. Due to the availability issues of lions, the Black Knight is now riding a fearsome ostrich!

PERCIVAL/GUINEVERE. Arrghh!

BLACK KNIGHT. Now, what do you say to my hand, Guinevere?

GUINEVERE. I say this.

She draws her sword. She sword-fights the BLACK KNIGHT. *Every time* PERCIVAL *attempts to help out,* GUINEVERE *instructs him to...*

Back off!

PERCIVAL *continues to try and help but gets more and more tangled in ropes, pots and pans, cymbals – anything that clashes and clangs.*

PERCIVAL. Don't you worry, Guinevere. I've got this.

Eventually GUINEVERE *captures the* BLACK KNIGHT*'s sword and has it to his throat.*

(*Tangled up in knots.*) Yes! We got him.

GUINEVERE. Swear on your life that you will never EVER ask for my hand again.

BLACK KNIGHT. Forgive me. I was paid a handsome figure to win you.

GUINEVERE. By whom? Speak or die!

BLACK KNIGHT. Morgana le Fay.

GUINEVERE. Morgana le Fay you say?

BLACK KNIGHT. I do say Morgana le Fay.

GUINEVERE. Then go away!

PERCIVAL *has worked himself free.*

PERCIVAL. And let that be a lesson to you. Now clear off!

The BLACK KNIGHT *exits.*

Are you hurt? No. Nasty piece of work. That's not the first time I've had to deal with him. Listen, I think we may have got off on the wrong foot. Might I take this opportunity to ask what you're doing tonight?

GUINEVERE *punches him in the face.*

Sure, no, look, you sound busy. How about Tuesday night?

ARTHUR *enters.*

GUINEVERE. Hello.

ARTHUR. Hello.

There's huge chemistry in the air, signified with music.

PERCIVAL. Er, excuse me.

ARTHUR/GUINEVERE. Shut up, Percival.

PERCIVAL. Who the hell do you think you are?!

ARTHUR. The one true King of England.

ARTHUR *raises his foot to place it dramatically on PERCIVAL's stool, but then realises he is still wearing one of the ostrich feet. He quickly removes it and throws it offstage.*

PERCIVAL. Blimey! Your gracious-ship. The one true King of England.

PERCIVAL *attempts to bow and curtsy at the same time.*

ARTHUR. Goodbye, Percival.

PERCIVAL. Yeah, just before I goodbye, could I just ask you something? I heard that you're looking for knights and well, I was just wondering…

ARTHUR. Yes, fine, granted.

PERCIVAL (*as if the suggestion hasn't already come from him*). Sorry? You're making me a knight?

ARTHUR. Yes, whatever!

PERCIVAL. Amazing! But don't you have to do the whole –

ARTHUR. OH MY GOD! FINE!

He does the knighting ceremony in, like, two seconds.

PERCIVAL. Sweet. I'll just… see you in Camelot!

PERCIVAL *exits.* ARTHUR *is finally alone with the beautiful* GUINEVERE.

ARTHUR. I was just wondering.

GUINEVERE. Yes?

ARTHUR. What're you doing for the rest of your life?

ARTHUR *tries to casually throw the stool off into the wings but it hits the set. The* SM *retrieves it.*

GUINEVERE. Wow.

ARTHUR. Too direct?

GUINEVERE. No. I love direct. But I must tell you something: Morgana le Fay was mixed up in this Black Knight business.

ARTHUR. My sister again? What's her game?

GUINEVERE. Perhaps to prevent us from meeting and becoming…

ARTHUR. Go ahead. Say it.

GUINEVERE. An item.

Stable door opens and smacks ARTHUR *in the face.* OSBERT *is playing the tune to 'Careless Whisper' (over a backing track) on the recorder, very badly.* ARTHUR *slams door shut.*

ARTHUR. Yes. Although I would never treat you as an item.

OSBERT *opens door again. 'Careless Whisper' on the recorder.*

Camelot will be a forward-thinking place of equality, where everyone has equal agency to have choice in the choices of agency.

GUINEVERE. That's a lot of buzzwords.

ARTHUR. I'm a buzzy person. Do you feel the buzz?

GUINEVERE. Everywhere. I feel like anything is possible.

ARTHUR *finally slams stable door on* OSBERT *again. But now the slider hatch opens, revealing* OSBERT*'s face as he continues to play.*

ARTHUR. Freedom in both body, mind… and heart?

GUINEVERE. That's three things.

ARTHUR. I like things in threes.

GUINEVERE. Are you talking about throuple relationships?

ARTHUR. I don't know. Am I?

GUINEVERE. Perhaps.

ARTHUR *hits* OSBERT *in the face with a plank and closes the hatch.* OSBERT *opens the top of the stable door. The recorder is in his throat. He pukes it out and continues playing.* EDGAR *breaks recorder in half and throws it in the stable.* OSBERT *looks very sad and* EDGAR *closes the door. The audience (always): 'Awwwww.'*

EDGAR. Okay, you want more recorder? Fine! Osbert?

EDGAR *opens the door to reveal* OSBERT *halfway through a costume change, mooning the audience, and quickly closes it.*

ARTHUR. You're just so damn modern. With you at my side we can change the world.

GUINEVERE. Then let's begin now.

ARTHUR. But Guinevere, I just need to say something first.

GUINEVERE. Say it, Arthur!

ARTHUR. In private, I mean.

GUINEVERE. We can tell each other anything.

EDGAR. You have to do a costume change.

DAVE. Ah yes.

DAVE *exits.* ARTHUR *addresses the audience with underscore still going.*

ARTHUR. What a flame has been ignited. Both in my own heart and in the heart of Camelot. A beacon of hope, of goodness, that upholds truth and fans the fair winds of justice. And so it was written, 'The Tale of Percival and the Black Knight'.

SFX: 'The Legend of Percival and the Black Knight' jingle.

Now onwards, with this amazing woman by my side, in search of my next knight. But what are my sister Morgana and her son Mordred really up to?

Scene Twenty-Five – Caravana Morgana

MORDRED *enters and is attempting to play Thrust Cup. It's the same principal as the ball-and-cup game (swinging a ball on a string into a cup) except the cup is attached to a belt around his waist and the ball is hanging from a string between his legs.*

MORDRED. Mother, I don't think your plans to stop Arthur from collecting knights and strengthening his court seem to be working. You should be thwarting them and yet, they are thwarting you!

MORGANA *enters.*

MORGANA. I'm perfectly well aware of that, Mordred. Now will you stop playing Thrust Cup. No one needs to see you cupping your ball all day. You're useless!

MORDRED. Sorry, Mother.

MORGANA. You're no help at all.

(*Singing to an arrangement of the jazz standard 'Caravan'.*)
Things have always gone so wrong for me
I should have been queen rightfully
Instead my home's a caravan

MORDRED. Oh, it's not all that bad.

MORGANA (*singing*).
How… can I pretend it doesn't hurt?
And so my choice is to pervert
The course of justice with a plan

MORDRED. A plan? Tell me, Mother!

MORGANA (*singing*).
This is so exciting
I will summon lightning
Day will turn to night, as I call
On the physical prowess of you!

MORDRED. Me?!

MORGANA (*singing*).
You'll use your talents in kung fu

MORDRED. But I'm only a yellow belt –

MORGANA (*singing*).
> My dream to rule is coming true
> My son will be the middle man

She does an insane laugh.

MORDRED (*singing*).
> Mum, Mum, Mum, Mum! Am I hearing you quite right?
> I challenge Arthur to a fight
> I really don't think that I can

MORGANA (*singing*).
> Son, son, son, son, although there's panic in your voice
> Have faith this is the only choice
> To help us leave our caravan

BOTH (*singing*).
> This is so exciting
> We will summon lightning
> We will rule the world, as we take
> What has always been rightfully mine
> King Arthur's running out of time
> We'll be the first ones in the line
> When he's dead we'll ditch our…
> Car-a-vaaan!

OSBERT (*sotto*). That was awesome, Dave! Nice one.

DAVE (*sotto*). Yeah, get off. (*To audience.*) Your Majesty. People of Camelot. We now present for you: 'The Legend of the Lady of Shalott'.

SFX: 'The Legend of the Lady of Shalott' jingle.

Scene Twenty-Six – Sir Lancelot and the Lady of Shalott

LANCELOT *enters on a horse, singing tunelessly to himself.*

LANCELOT (*singing*).
I'm riding through the countryside, the countryside, the countryside, I'm riding through the countryside, all day lerng.

Suddenly his horse is spooked.

Whoa boy, whoa! What 'as got you all worked urp, Gringolet?! Something weird seems to be 'appening to zis 'orse! Even zo I am a professional, I feel I may fall orf. Calm down, Gringolet, Lancelot cannot be booked orf!

GRINGOLET (*voice-over*). I'm doing my best, mate, but when I'm spooked, I'm spooked.

LANCELOT. Oh. You can talk? Why 'ave you never talked before?

GRINGOLET (*voice-over*). Never felt the urge, to be fair. But there's something flipping dodgy going on in that tower.

LANCELOT. Oh. I'd better go and take a look.

GRINGOLET (*voice-over*). Oh give it a rest, not another heroic act. A damsel in distress? So predictable. The problem is, the notion of chivalry reinforces the patriarchy. Can we please just get to Camelot so you can present yourself to the king?!

LANCELOT. You speak the truth but I don't like it! I need to get off with you! Off you! Get me off! Now! Yah!

They exit. Instrumental music. The LADY OF SHALOTT *appears, sitting in a bathtub with baked beans dripping over the sides.* (*NB. The actor is in a naked suit with baked beans strategically placed.*)

SHALOTT. Help! Someone please help me! I'm trapped in this tower and the whole village of Astolat has been held hostage.

LANCELOT (*off*). Hello?

SHALOTT. Who's there?

He appears below.

LANCELOT. My name is Lancelot du Lac.

SHALOTT. Ooh, you're very chiselled.

LANCELOT. Oui. And I shall untrap you.

SHALOTT. But the door is guarded by a fearsome dragon.

Door at the bottom of the tower opens to reveal DAVE *in a rubbish dragon costume.*

LANCELOT. Then I will slay this dragon and release you.

SHALOTT. Oh it's more complicated than that. I'm cursed.

LANCELOT. A curse? What kind of curse?

SHALOTT. To be trapped in a bath of boiling baked beans.

LANCELOT. What kind of crazy sicko would do zat?!

SHALOTT. Morgana le Fay.

LANCELOT. Zat woman! What is 'er problem?! Do not move! Out of my way, dragon, and prepare to die!

He defeats the DRAGON *with some bad wrestling followed by* LANCELOT *breaking the* DRAGON*'s neck. He then scales the wall up to the tower window and climbs through.*

Okay, I'm attempting to avert my eyes. I want you to try to get out of the bath.

SHALOTT. Impossible. I'm stuck.

LANCELOT. My summation is that you have just been hypnotised to *think* zat you are stook. Also, that these beans could do with a drop of Worcestershire sauce.

SHALOTT. Well what can you do? I've been boiling for a month and a day.

LANCELOT. Okay. I'm averting my eyes from your bodey but I want you to look into my eyes.

SHALOTT. They're so blue.

LANCELOT. Oui.

SHALOTT. So gorgeous.

LANCELOT. Oui. Now when I cloock ma foongers you will simply get out of the bath.

LANCELOT *clicks his fingers.* LADY OF SHALOTT *gets out.*

Et voilà!

SHALOTT. Oh. I'm free!

LANCELOT. I'm averting my eyes. Do you have a tool?

SHALOTT. What, like a screwdriver?

LANCELOT. No, a tool. A nice floofy tool.

SHALOTT. Oh, you mean a towel. (*Teaching him to pronounce.*) Ta.

LANCELOT. Twa.

SHALOTT. Ta.

LANCELOT. Twa.

SHALOTT. Wel.

LANCELOT. Woooool.

SHALOTT. Towel.

LANCELOT. Tool.

SHALOTT. Forget the towel! You saved me!

LANCELOT. No, do not hurg me, your boobies are all boeany!

SHALOTT. And I love you.

A love theme begins.

LANCELOT. Oh, sacre bleu.

SHALOTT. And if you say that you can't love me back then I might as well get back in the bath!

LANCELOT. D'accord. Au revoir.

GUINEVERE *enters from below.*

GUINEVERE. Hello? Who's up there? Reveal yourself. I said reveal yourself!

LANCELOT. And who demands it?! You, pass me that window.

LADY OF SHALOTT *passes him a windowframe from off the wall, which he looks out of. It's love at first sight.*

GUINEVERE. My name is Guinevere.

LANCELOT. And mine is Lancelot.

SHALOTT (*grabbing the window*). And mine is the Lady of Shalott!

GUINEVERE. Sorry, I seem to have interrupted some kind of –

LANCELOT (*taking the window back*). No, it's nothing.

SHALOTT. Marry me!

LANCELOT. She's emotional. She's been boiled in beans for over a month.

GUINEVERE. Ouch.

LANCELOT. What can I do for you?

GUINEVERE. I'm looking for the king.

LANCELOT. King Arthur?! Me too! I'll come and assist you.

He races down to GUINEVERE. *They start to exit.*

SHALOTT. No! Come back or I'll… put a curse on you to make you believe *I am* that woman.

LANCELOT *races back, furious, pointing.*

LANCELOT. Do not put a curse on me! I've just saved your life!

SHALOTT. But I can't live without you!

LANCELOT. You need to find a more suitable partener, like someone made of toast. So you can spread your boeany boobies all over their boody. (*To audience.*) And as a point of interest, beans on toast is the only English dish I have any respect for. Why? Because the recipe is in the title. Au revoir!

LANCELOT *exits.* LADY OF SHALOTT *is grief-stricken but, when she realises it's too late, she is suddenly fine and says…*

OSBERT. And that my friends, is 'The Legend of the Lady of Shalott'.

SFX: 'The Legend of the Lady of Shalott' jingle. OSBERT *exits.* MORGANA *enters.*

MORGANA. Noooooo! How did a woman in a boiling bath of baked beans, trapped in a tower, fail to prevent Lancelot ever meeting Arthur?! It's time I take matters into my own hands. Time for me to use my powers of disguise.

Creepy child-catcher music. MORGANA *takes on her disguise as the ice-cream seller.*

Scene Twenty-Seven – Ice Creams

MORGANA (*as ice-cream seller*). Getta your tutsi frutzi ice-a-creams. Ice creams. Anything you could wish for, all the flavours your heart might desire. All here waiting for you. Come and get your ice cream!

ARTHUR *enters.*

ARTHUR. What is Morgana up to? I must find her. Wow. What a friendly looking ice-cream seller! A sweet treat – just what I need. Hello, what flavours have you got?

MORGANA (*as ice-cream seller*). All the flavours under the sun.

ARTHUR. Okay, vanilla?

MORGANA (*as ice-cream seller*). No.

ARTHUR. Strawberry?

MORGANA (*as ice-cream seller*). No.

ARTHUR. Chocolate?

MORGANA (*as ice-cream seller*). No.

ARTHUR. Raspberry ripple?

MORGANA (*as ice-cream seller*). Yes!

ARTHUR. One raspberry ripple please!

MORGANA (*as ice-cream seller*). Of course! That's a nice sword.

ARTHUR. Yes – Excalibur! The greatest sword in the world.

MORGANA (*as ice-cream seller*). Three groats please.

ARTHUR (*attempting to reach his pockets*). Okay, just a second.

MORGANA (*as ice-cream seller*). I'll hold your sword for you.

ARTHUR. Oh, thank you.

He hands his sword to MORGANA (*as the ice-cream seller*), *who swaps Excalibur with another sword and hides Excalibur behind her.* ARTHUR *turns back to her, having found his money.*

Here you are. Three groats?

MORGANA (*as ice-cream seller*). Yes. Enjoy your ice cream.

ARTHUR. Thank you.

He goes to leave.

MORGANA (*as ice-cream seller*). Don't forget your sword.

She hands ARTHUR *the fake sword.*

ARTHUR. Oh yes! Many thanks! Yummy! Raspberry ripple. Delicious.

He exits. MORGANA *reveals herself.*

MORGANA. Hello, Excalibur! Now then, children, who wants an ice cream? You would like one, would you? Well you can't. They aren't real. They're props. They're just empty pots glued together. Ha, ha! Time for my next disguise!

She exits.

Scene Twenty-Eight – Balyn and Balan

Enter BALYN and BALAN to a Scottish jig. They are wearing identical tunics and, importantly, the same family crest. They're Scottish.

BALAN. I'm Balyn.

BALYN. And I'm Balan. Wait, is that right?

BALAN. No, we've got it wrong again. Excuse us.

They exit and re-enter and switch.

BALYN. I'm Balyn.

BALAN. And so is he. So am I?!

BALYN. He's Balan.

BALAN. And he's Balyn.

BOTH. And this is 'The Legend of Balyn and Balan'.

SFX: 'The Legend of Balyn and Balan' jingle. They shake hands.

BALYN. I'll see you later, brother. I'm going to look for something chivalrous to do.

BALAN. Alright, catch you later, pal. I'm going to look for something chivalrous too.

BALYN exits. BALAN turns on the spot. Enter MORGANA as Lady Lyle. Instrumental music. She has a sword sticking out of her stomach.

Alright, madame?

MORGANA (*as Lady Lyle*). Hello. A lot of weather we've been having recently.

BALAN. Yeah.

MORGANA (*as Lady Lyle*). Off anywhere nice?

BALAN. No, not in particular. Look, I don't mean to be impolite but you appear to have a sword skewering your abdomen.

MORGANA (*as Lady Lyle*). Yep.

BALAN. Would you not like it removed?

MORGANA (*as Lady Lyle*). Most certainly. But it can only be removed by someone valiant and true of heart. And to be honest there aren't many of those around.

BALAN. Well, you're in luck, madame.

MORGANA (*as Lady Lyle*). Really?

BALAN. Aye. Let me try.

She presents her belly. BALAN *prepares himself and pulls it out.*

MORGANA (*as Lady Lyle*). Aaargghh! That's… you've done it! I am forever indebted to you.

BALAN. Don't worry about it, love. Wow! Nice piece.

MORGANA (*as Lady Lyle*). Yes. Although of course it's cursed and therefore must be destroyed.

BALAN. That's a bit extreme.

MORGANA (*as Lady Lyle*). Believe me, if you keep this sword, you *will* destroy that which you love most in the world. Now hand it over.

BALAN. Why would I do that?! Me – a man who has just proved himself to be valiant and true of heart.

MORGANA (*aside to audience*). And stupid too, it would seem.

BALAN. What was that?

MORGANA (*as Lady Lyle*). Nothing.

He produces his own sword.

BALAN. I will be known as the man with two swords. Everyone from America to China will know my name, madame. Two swords.

MORGANA (*as Lady Lyle*). Well I tried. What can you do?

(*Aside to audience.*) Time for my final disguise.

BALAN. What was that?

MORGANA (*as Lady Lyle*). I said time for my… I mean nothing.

She exits.

BALAN. But my family crest should reflect my new persona. I shall seek out a tailor to design me a crest with two crossed swords. I love crossing swords.

ITALIAN TAILOR enters. He places a new family crest with two crossed swords onto BALAN. He speaks incredibly fast while he does this.

MORGANA. Allora ragazzi, penne al pomodoro, spaghetti frutti di mare, tiramisù e cannoli. Ciao!

He swiftly exits.

BALAN. I love it! Onwards. What could possibly go wrong?!

He performs a 'Scottish dance'. MORGANA *in disguise as Madame Riddler enters pushing a very large wooden/cardboard packaging case. She then sits beside it on a three-legged stool and pours from a flask of tea.*

Afternoon.

MORGANA (*as Madame Riddler*). Afternoon.

BALAN. That's a big box.

MORGANA (*as Madame Riddler*). Yep.

BALAN. Yours?

MORGANA (*as Madame Riddler*). Might be.

Something inside the box kicks.

BALAN. What have you got in there?

MORGANA (*as Madame Riddler*).
You wish to know what's in the box?
A strange and curious beast in socks.

BALAN. Well, it's kind of blocking the path, love. Do you wanna move it?

MORGANA (*as Madame Riddler*).
I will give thought to what you ask.
But not until I've drained this flask.

BALAN *draws his sword.*

BALAN. Or perhaps before?

MORGANA (*as Madame Riddler*).
If you can guess what lies within,
I'll move it now and you will win.

BALAN. Oh God. Okay, fine. A giant wombat?

MORGANA (*as Madame Riddler*). Nope. Two more guesses.

BALAN. Two more guesses?!

MORGANA (*as Madame Riddler*). Out of three.

BALAN. Or what?!

MORGANA (*as Madame Riddler*). Or you have to fight it.

BALAN. Are you insane?

MORGANA (*as Madame Riddler*). Close. I'm a Riddler.

She does the Riddler dance to a burst of music.

BALAN (*suddenly very panicked*). You're a Riddler?!

MORGANA *does the Riddler dance.*

MORGANA (*as Madame Riddler*). Ha ha ha ha ha! (*She turns nasty.*) Next guess!

BALAN (*very scared*). Tell you what. I'll just find another route.

MORGANA (*as Madame Riddler*). Stop!
Walk away, things will be worse,
Keep on guessing or receive a curse!

BALAN. You can't just introduce a curse.

MORGANA (*as Madame Riddler*). Yes I can, I'm a Riddler!

MORGANA *does the Riddler dance then falls off her stool when she sits. Composes herself.*

Guess!

BALAN. A giant wombat? Oh flip I've said that.

MORGANA (*as Madame Riddler*). Too bad! Final chance!!
Ha ha ha!!

BALAN. Something completely different. A fruit bat?! What is wrong with me! Come on, Batman, I mean Balyn! No! Balan! What's my name?!

MORGANA (*as Madame Riddler*). Wrong again. And now you must fight it.

BALAN. The fruit bat?!

MORGANA (*as Madame Riddler, spoken with slow menace*). No! An invisi-bull bull-lock! Ha ha!

BALAN. An invisa bulbul lock?!

MORGANA (*as Madame Riddler*). No, an invisible bull-lock.

BALAN. A what?!

MORGANA (*as Madame Riddler*). A bullock that's invisible!

BALAN. Then release your bullock, madame.

MORGANA (*as Madame Riddler*). Oh no no no! That'd be a lot less fun. For its invisibility is contained within the box. Outside the box it's just a normal bull. It's a box fight!

BALAN. A box fight?!

MORGANA (*as Madame Riddler*). Like a cage fight, except it's in a box.

BALAN. This is so weird. But whatever. For I am Two-Swords Balan and I will destroy whatever's in that box. How do I get in?

MORGANA (*as Madame Riddler*).
Through the door, it's on the side...

BALAN *heads through the door.*

...You'll find within it's tall and wide.

BALAN (*from inside box*). It's not. It's a tiny wee box! It's small and dark. I can't see a flipping thing. And where's the bull?!

Much moo-ing. Wild-bull SFX and kicking. Bull horns and hooves and sword ends rip through the walls of the box. It's carnage within but eventually BALAN *crawls out. The* MORGANA *as Madame Riddler laughs.*

Whatever that was, it won't live long. I have slain the bull-beast because I am Two-Swords Balan.

MORGANA (*as Madame Riddler*). Hahaha!

ACT TWO, SCENE TWENTY-EIGHT

BALAN. What's so funny?

MORGANA (*as Madame Riddler*).
 The bull, you fool, was just a cover,
 The fight you had was with your brother.

 BALYN *enters, screaming, with a dagger, and stabs* BALAN.

 Warned you were, the sword was cursed,
 How foolish but, you're not the first.

 MORGANA *as Madame Riddler exits. Instrumental music.*

BALYN. Ach no, brother! If only I had known it was you. But how could I recognise you? You'd changed your coat of arms.

BALAN. I forgive you!

BOTH. We shared a womb. And now a tomb!

They both die, leaning against each other in counterbalance. Then are instantly revived.

BALYN. And yet all was not lost.

BALAN. Because this miraculous story has a further twist in its tail.

BALYN. For it both happened and didn't happen.

BOTH. Simultaneously.

BALAN. King Arthur knighted us and granted us the opportunity to recount it –

 Again and again. And that, folks, is 'The Legend of Balyn and Balan'.

SFX: 'The Legend of Balyn and Balan' jingle. They exit.
MORGANA *appears.*

MORGANA. What?! How can they survive?! And how can an event both happen and not happen? This land has no parameters of logic! I will bring my ultimate plan forward… to now.

She exits.

Scene Twenty-Nine – The Final Battle

OSBERT *enters, dressed as King Arthur, and places a makeshift wooden throne.*

OSBERT. Your Majesty, people of Camelot, we now present to you our final legend. 'The Legend of'… 'The Legend of'…

EDGAR (*poking head out*). 'The Final Legend'!

OSBERT. 'The Legend of the Final Legend of the Legend of King Arthur'.

SFX: 'The Legend of King Arthur' jingle. OSBERT *puts on the crown to become* ARTHUR. LANCELOT *enters.*

LANCELOT. Sire, you are in danger. I taste it in the air, it's like an oeuf that's gone off.

ARTHUR. Where's Guinevere?

GUINEVERE (*off*). Coming!

LANCELOT. Arthur, we must get you to safety.

ARTHUR. Really? Somewhere away from you and my betrothed perhaps?

LANCELOT. Excuse me?

ARTHUR. Don't take me for a fool, Lancelot. I've seen the looks between you both.

LANCELOT. Sire! You have nothing to fear. Trust me. Nothing's going on!

ARTHUR. Nothing *yet*, perhaps. But it's only a matter of time before you'll be hammering away like couple of –

GUINEVERE *enters.*

GUINEVERE. Arthur!

ARTHUR. What?!

GUINEVERE. I don't find him *unattractive*, it's true. I'd be lying if I said I did. But don't try to tell me you don't find other people attractive.

She turns to the audience.

What person here, currently in a relationship, can honestly say you haven't fantasised about someone else in, say, the last week. In fact, raise your hand if you *haven't* had that fantasy?! You see. No raised hands – they're all at it!

She picks on an audience member.

Excuse me, madame, would you care to share your fantasy with the group?

ARTHUR. Okay! I get it. It's just a lot to take on board, that's all. But I vow to be a king who understands his people, who strives not to be hypocritical and breed dysfunctionality through a system of repressive hierarchy.

EDGAR *starts to realise where this is heading and tries to make* OSBERT *stop.*

Camelot will be a new type of civilisation where every person will be equal and that equality will be a legacy that will echo throughout eternity! Down with the monarchy!

EDGAR. Osbert, no! Not that!

OSBERT. I mean, long live the king! Woo!

GUINEVERE. Arthur, your enemy approaches.

ARTHUR. My enemy?

LANCELOT. Mordred.

ARTHUR. Mordred?! Where?

Both look at OSBERT. *He quickly gives his Arthur costume to* EDGAR *and runs off.*

EDGAR *and* DAVE *have to fill while they wait for* OSBERT *to quick-change into* MORDRED.

GUINEVERE. Arthur, your enemy approaches.

ARTHUR. My enemy?

GUINEVERE. Mordred.

ARTHUR. Mordred?! Where?

GUINEVERE. There.

MORDRED *enters.*

MORDRED. Father.

ARTHUR. I think you mean Uncle.

MORDRED. Oh, the jury's out on that.

ARTHUR. What?! Oh God, that means –

MORDRED. Yes. That your time has come.

ARTHUR. No, *your* time has come

MORDRED. No, *your* time has come.

ARTHUR. Enough! We can discuss this reasonably. Because you will never win against – (*Drawing his sword.*) Excalibur.

MORDRED. If that is indeed Excalibur and wasn't swapped when you bought a raspberry-ripple ice cream from my mother disguised as an ice-cream seller!

He presents the real Excalibur and thrusts it high in the air.

ARTHUR. No! How could I have been such a fool?! The allure of a sweet deception!

ARTHUR *and* MORDRED *fight.* ARTHUR *is wounded, but Excalibur is eventually won from* MORDRED. ARTHUR *kills* MORDRED.

MORDRED. I die!

ARTHUR (*sotto*). Not there.

MORDRED. I die!

ARTHUR (*sotto*). A little further off.

MORDRED. I die!

ARTHUR (*sotto*). Oh, and take the throne with you.

MORDRED. I die. Offstage apparently.

Exit MORDRED *with throne.* GUINEVERE *rushes to* ARTHUR*'s side. Instrumental music.*

GUINEVERE. Arthur! Can you hear me?

ARTHUR. It is over, my love. Slain by my own sword! You must take this – (*Hands her Excalibur.*) and throw it into the Lady of the Lake Lake.

She gathers him in her arms.

GUINEVERE. Of course.

ARTHUR. Guinevere, I'm sorry.

GUINEVERE. What for?

ARTHUR. For not making the world a better place.

He dies.

GUINEVERE. No! You can't die. You *must* make the world a better place!

SFX: wind, a storm brewing and MERLIN'*s voice echoes over the top.*

MERLIN (*voice-over*). And he will.

GUINEVERE. But how?!

She exits.

Blackout with searchlights – where is Merlin? During the following dialogue, OSBERT *appears on the platform above* ARTHUR *and he throws white rose petals down over him. They get stuck to his hands so he eventually ends up dispensing the entire box contents in one go.*

MERLIN. I come through the darkness of time. I am the light of life. The genesis of a story, the end of a bell. I am a dominator of space, a creator of tricks… I am a… Dom… ina… trix.

MERLIN *appears from the fog and starts to sing.*

(*Singing.*) How can I… reverse the time?
I need to… turn back the clock
Arthur, it's not your time to leave us
So let's rock!

A bit of this, a bit of that
A long white beard and a pointy hat
A magic spell will help you breathe
Just feel the power from my wizard's sleeve

MERLIN *discards his cloak to reveal a leotard.* ARTHUR *is brought back to life – aghast.*

It's time for resurrection
It's time for life once more
You are a legend, Arthur, so baby…

How can I reverse the time?
I need to turn back the clock
Arthur, it's not your time to leave us
So let's rock!

Over the following dialogue, OSBERT *enters with Excalibur and presents it to* ARTHUR. ARTHUR *draws it, cutting* OSBERT*'s hands in doing so.*

(*Spoken.*) Arthur, it is not yet your time to pass into the next life. You have much to do! With Guinevere and your Knights of the Round Table you must rule over Camelot, the most just kingdom the world has ever known and become… a Legend.

ALL (*singing*).
How can I reverse the time?
I need to turn back the clock
Arthur, it's not your time to leave us
So let's rock!
Let's rock!

ARTHUR *is raised up. It's an OTT, full-on Cher stage-show ending. The three* SQUIRES *bow. End of the show-within-a-show.*

EDGAR. Your Majesty, good people of Camelot, you have been watching *The Legends of King Arthur*! Thank you and goodnight.

SFX: 'The Legend of King Arthur' jingle.

Scene Thirty – Post-Show Backstage

The sound of applause/atmos fades. DAVE *and* EDGAR *strike the tent during the following.*

DAVE. Edgar, we did it! How do you think it went?

EDGAR. I think we tried our absolute best.

DAVE. And that's the main thing. Even though King Arthur looked pretty red in the face at the end.

EDGAR. And had his fists clenched.

DAVE. Which could have been in pleasure.

EDGAR. Yep. Or anger. Hard to tell.

ARTHUR (*off*). Where are they?! Well the hell are they?!

DAVE. Just as *that* could be the voice of exuberance.

EDGAR. Yep. Or anger. Just nipping to the loo.

DAVE. What?!

EDGAR *quickly exits.* ARTHUR *enters.*

ARTHUR. How dare you! Magic wizards? A lake lady? Baths of beans? Headless giants? Invisi-bull-bulls whatever. And whatever this is!

He pings DAVE*'s leotard.*

DAVE. Oh this? This is art.

ARTHUR. You really think this utter nonsense is the kind of acts that the King of England would award knighthoods for?!

DAVE. I can imagine less deserving people receiving peerages in the future.

ARTHUR. Enough! You have made a laughing stock of me. Any street cred I had has been obliterated! And therefore, you and your friends will be placed in stocks and sentenced to a slow and painful death. Guard! Take them away. And get everyone to throw rotten veg at them.

Instrumental music.

Scene Thirty-One – Court

SM *enters and displays a sign – 'Later that day...'* ARTHUR *enters and is pacing. Furious.*

ARTHUR. How could they? The sheer audacity of it. Making me look more stupid than I already am.

A GUARD, *enters.*

GUARD. Your Majesty?

ARTHUR. What is it?!

GUARD *has a quiet but lengthy word in* ARTHUR*'s ear.*

ARTHUR. Really? Seriously? No way. You've got to be… blimey, uh-ha… uh-ha… uh-ha… a-ha-ha-ha… a-huh-huh-huh oh yeah, that's the way a-ha, a-ha… I like it a-ha a-ha. I like it a lot! Get Dave in here immediately!

GUARD *exits and enters with* DAVE (*in stocks*).

Dave! I believe I owe you a huge apology. Apparently, your show has prompted a queue of a thousand wannabe knights outside the castle walls who all profess to swear allegiance to me and Camelot if I deem their stories to be worthy!

DAVE. Say what?

GUARD. The consensus amongst them is that they've never been so inspired to serve a right and proper king.

DAVE. That is insane!

GUARD *hands Excalibur to* ARTHUR.

ARTHUR. Kneel.

DAVE. It's Dave actually.

ARTHUR. Well, Dave Actually. I hereby knight you, Sir Dave.

DAVE. No sorry, could I just stop you there. I have long coveted the title Sir Dave the Rave.

ARTHUR. Then I bestow upon you the title of Sir Dave the Rave.

Knighting fanfare.

Have you anything you'd like to say?

ACT TWO, SCENE THIRTY-ONE

DAVE. Just one thing. Camelot, make some noise!

A big rave anthem drops. DAVE *releases himself from the stocks and celebrates.*

ARTHUR *and* GUARD *dance off, leaving* DAVE *lost in his own world, rapping to the underscore. The music transitions to the sound of pots and pans being bashed and he's back in the farmyard.* OSBERT *and* EDGAR *enter.*

OSBERT. Dave, Dave!

EDGAR. Dave!

OSBERT. Cut the music!

EDGAR hits DAVE over the head with a tray. Music cuts.

DAVE. Alright losers. And B-T-dubs, it's Sir Dave the Rave now. I've been knighted.

BOTH. What?

DAVE. Yeah! Where have you been?

OSBERT. In the stocks up until two minutes ago.

DAVE. Oh yeah, my bad – forgot to pass on the message to release you. Apparently our show was a massive junglist hit.

EDGAR. Yeah we heard. So, what about *our* knighthoods?

DAVE. All sorted. Well, kind of.

OSBERT. What do you mean kind of?

DAVE. There's just one condition.

OSBERT. *What* condition?

DAVE. Well, after a pint… or maybe ten with the king… I might have said we'd come up with a few more stories.

EDGAR. How many more?!

DAVE. Like… a thousand?

OSBERT. A thousand?!

EDGAR and OSBERT head upstage to fetch the frying pan and a plank of wood.

DAVE. I was drunk. People say stuff when they're drunk!

EDGAR. Dave, you absolute…

They go to smack DAVE *in the face with the pan and plank but freeze with SFX sting. Lights out. Flashing searchlights over the set. The end? Not quite. A vamp a bit like the intro of 'December, 1963 (Oh, What a Night)' by The Four Seasons begins. Over this vamp a recorded voice says the following:*

VOICE. And so it was written. The three squires of Camelot went on to write thousands of stories that became absolutely legendary.

Edgar cashed in on the squires' home-brewed beer, setting up a farmyard brewery so popular that even Lancelot served it in his restaurant. Osbert attended Bill Spollock's twelve-week acting workshop. He enjoyed it so much that they then went on to form a company together. Spolbert's Theatre Ensemble. Dave's DJ career took the world by storm. He took an early retirement and now has his own successful line of glow sticks. HashtagDaveSticks. And that, my friends, is 'The Legend of the Legendary Legends of Three Squires Who Went on to Become Great Knights'.

EDGAR *appears on top stage-left platform in silver-sequinned hotpants and tank top, silver Crocs and a silver knight's helmet. He sings…*

EDGAR (*singing*).
  Now I'm a knight
  It started way back in five-oh-three

DAVE (*singing*).
  A.D.!

EDGAR (*singing*).
  Such a very crazy time it's been

DAVE (*singing*).
  We're free!

EDGAR (*singing*).
  Look at me now
  I'm a knight!

OSBERT *appears on top stage-left platform in an outfit identical to* EDGAR. *They join in with the song.*

OSBERT (*singing*).
  Now I'm a knight

EDGAR (*singing*).
  So fresh!

OSBERT (*singing*).
  I spent my life being a lowly squire

EDGAR (*singing*).
  So peak!

OSBERT (*singing*).
  But now I can get what I desire
  Because I made it
  I'm a knight!

DAVE *appears centre-stage in the same outfit as the others.*

DAVE (*singing*).
  And I, I saved us all from an early grave
  And now, I'm living my best life as Sir Dave –

ALL (*singing*).
  The Rave!
  Now I'm a knight!
  Now I'm a knight!
  Now I'm a knight!
  Now I'm a knight!
  Now we're all knights!

They form a still pose together at the front of the stage in a single spotlight as the lights fade.

The End.

www.nickhernbooks.co.uk

@nickhernbooks